BREAKING
100
90
80

Taking Your Game to the Next Level
with the Best Teachers in Golf

BREAKING
100
90
80

Edited by Scott Smith
and the Staff of

GolfDigest

DOUBLEDAY
New York London Toronto Sydney Auckland

PUBLISHED BY DOUBLEDAY
a division of Random House, Inc.

DOUBLEDAY and the portrayal of an anchor with a dolphin are registered trademarks of
Random House, Inc.

• • •

Book design by Judy Turziano

• • •

FRONTIS ART
title page: England's Gary Evans celebrates a clutch putt at the 2002 British Open.
contents page: Left: Annika Sorenstam.
XI: Juli Inkster..

• • •

PHOTOGRAPHY CREDITS
All photography by *Golf Digest* staff photographers
Stephen Szurlej and Dom Furore unless otherwise noted.

Darron Carroll: 16–17, 196–197, 226–227, 229; J.D. Cuban: VIII, XII–1, 75, 124, 137, 141 (*right*),
158–159, 180–181, 187 (*left*), 193 (*upper*), 231 (*right*), 240–241, 261; Dee Darden: 37; Bob Ewell: 113, 273;
Bill Fields: 214; *Getty Images*: 206–207, 236; Sam Greenwood: 211; Jim Gund: 78, 80–81, 275; Scott Halleran: 260;
Rusty Jarrett: 108–109; Jim Moriarty: 7, 10, 13, 14 (*right*), 15, 16 (*left*), 18 (*left*), 21, 23, 24, 27, 34, 35 (*left*), 47, 49,
55, 57, 60 (*right*), 62, 63, 72, 73, 76, 77, 85, 87 (*upper*), 89, 90–91, 94, 106, 114 (*left*), 115, 117, 122, 123,
125, 126, 127, 138, 141, 147, 148, 152, 153, 163, 164 (*right*), 165, 166, 167, 168–169, 170, 172–173, 174, 184 (*upper*),
185, 189 (*right*), 190, 191 (*upper*), 194, 195 (*upper*), 198, 199, 202 (*upper*), 209, 216, 221, 233, 231 (*left*), 235, 237,
238–239, 244 (*left*), 245, 252–253, 262, 263, 270–271; Gary Newkirk: 18, 52–53, 150–151, 195, 204–205,
230, 234, 235, 242; Chris Stanford: 154–155, 171, 186, 187, 212, 222–223; Joey Terrill: 255, 269.

ILLUSTRATION CREDITS
Illustrated backgrounds by Jim Luft of *Luft & Leone Design*
Sam Ward: 5, 7, 9, 21, 30, 32, 35, 42, 45, 55, 57, 59, 61, 69, 73, 77, 89, 93, 106, 117, 119, 123,
124, 129, 131, 138, 147, 149, 152, 155, 163, 169, 171, 176, 185, 186, 191, 192, 198, 200, 202, 210, 213,
216, 219, 220, 233, 237, 238, 243, 245, 248, 257, 259, 260, 262, 266, 269; + *Ism*: 211.

• • •

The cataloging-in-publication data is on file with the Library of Congress
ISBN 0-385-51190-6

• • •

PRINTED IN THE UNITED STATES OF AMERICA
May 2004
First Edition
1 2 3 4 5 6 7 8 9 10

◆

*If we did all the things we
are capable of doing, we would
literally astonish ourselves.*

—Thomas Edison

◆

CONTENTS

CONTRIBUTORS

An all-star collection of swing tips, practice drills and game-management advice, *Breaking 100, 90, 80* features instructional help from today's top teachers and players, from David Leadbetter and Butch Harmon to Ernie Els and Justin Leonard. Throughout this book, these *Golf Digest* Teaching Professionals, Playing Editors, leading swing coaches and tour pros speak directly to you. Below are just some of the contributors; to find advice from specific players or instructors, turn to the Index on page 276 for tips categorized by person and by subject.

JANET COLES
A two-time winner on the LPGA Tour, Coles now teaches amateur golfers and elite junior players at Quail Lodge Resort & Golf Club in Carmel, Calif., and the Presidio Golf Course in San Francisco.

CHUCK COOK
Voted No. 7 by his peers in *Golf Digest's* ranking of America's 50 Greatest Teachers, Cook has worked with Payne Stewart and Tom Kite. He teaches at the Chuck Cook Golf Academies in Spicewood, Tex., and Wolcott, Colo.

JANE CRAFTER
A native of Perth, Australia, Crafter has competed on the LPGA Tour for more than 20 years. In 1987 she won the JCPenney Classic with Steve Jones, and in 1990 she won the LPGA's Phar-Mor at Inverrary tournament.

SCOTT DAVENPORT
Davenport is head golf professional at Quail Hollow Club in Charlotte, N.C., and a top-ranked teacher in that state. A longtime Golf Digest Schools instructor, Davenport has been contributing articles to Golf Digest since 1984.

ERNIE ELS
Els first gained acclaim by winning the world under-14 title in San Diego. Since 1992, he has won more than 40 professional tournaments worldwide, including the 1994 and 1997 U.S. Open Championships and the 2002 British Open.

HANK HANEY
A longtime *Golf Digest* Teaching Professional and No. 5 on the 50 Greatest Teachers list, Haney has taught Mark O'Meara, among other top pros. He owns and operates the Hank Haney Golf Ranch in McKinney, Tex.

BUTCH HARMON
Voted No. 1 by his peers in *Golf Digest's* ranking of America's 50 Greatest Teachers, Butch has coached Tiger Woods and many other top pros. He owns the Butch Harmon School of Golf at Rio Secco Golf Club in Henderson, Nev.

DAVID LEADBETTER
Voted No. 2 by his peers in *Golf Digest's* ranking of the 50 Greatest Teachers, Leadbetter operates 27 golf academies worldwide. Among the tour players he teaches are Ernie Els, Nick Price, Charles Howell III and Aaron Baddeley.

JUSTIN LEONARD
Winner of the 1997 British Open and 1998 Players Championship and two-time Ryder Cup member, Leonard also won the U.S. Amateur in 1992, and was an All-American at the University of Texas in 1993–'94.

JACK LUMPKIN
The 1995 PGA Teacher of the Year, Lumpkin is the longtime coach of Davis Love III. He first started teaching at Golf Digest Schools in 1976 and is currently director of instruction at Sea Island Golf Club in Georgia.

JIM McLEAN
The No. 3-ranked teacher on *Golf Digest*'s 50 Greatest Teachers list, McLean teaches Len Mattiace, among other tour pros. The Jim McLean Golf Schools are based at Doral Golf Resort and Spa in Miami.

JOHNNY MILLER
A dominant PGA Tour player during the 1970s, Miller is a longtime golf analyst for NBC and columnist for *Golf Digest*. He and his sons teach at the Johnny Miller Golf Academy, Palm Beach Polo, Golf & Country Club in West Palm Beach, Fla.

RANDY MYERS
The fitness director at PGA National Resort & Spa in Palm Beach Gardens, Fla., Myers trains more than 80 tour professionals, including Bruce Fleisher, Gary Player and Michelle McGann.

TOM NESS
A longtime instructor for Golf Digest Schools, Ness is the director of instruction at the Chateau Elan Winery and Resort in Braselton, Ga., and is one of *Golf Digest*'s 50 Greatest Teachers, as ranked by his peers.

NICK PRICE
Inducted into the World Golf Tour Hall of Fame in 2003, Price has won 18 times on the PGA Tour, starting with a defeat of Jack Nicklaus at the World Series of Golf in 1983. He's won two PGA Championships and one British Open.

JUDY RANKIN
A member of the LPGA Hall of Fame, Rankin was a two-time Player of the Year and won three Vare Trophy honors. A golf commentator for ABC, Rankin captained the victorious 1996 and '98 U.S. Solheim Cup Teams.

DEAN REINMUTH
One of *Golf Digest*'s 50 Greatest Teachers and a regular on The Golf Channel, Reinmuth is credited with helping Phil Mickelson's game since age 13. The Dean Reinmuth Golf Schools are based in San Diego.

DR. BOB ROTELLA
A former director of sport psychology at the University of Virginia, Rotella has worked with many tour pros and sports organizations. A *Golf Digest* Professional Advisor, he is also the author of such best-sellers as *Golf Is Not a Game of Perfect*.

RANDY SMITH
The 2003 PGA Teacher of the Year, Smith is head professional at Royal Oaks Country Club in Dallas. More than 150 juniors taught by Smith, including Justin Leonard, have received college golf scholarships.

RICK SMITH
No. 4 on *Golf Digest*'s 50 Greatest Teachers list, Smith has coached many tour players, including Phil Mickelson, Lee Janzen and Rocco Mediate. He teaches at the Treetops Resort in Gaylord, Mich., and Tiburon in Naples, Fla.

DAVID TOMS
Winner of the 2001 PGA Championship and seven PGA Tour titles, Toms led the 2002 U.S. Ryder Cup squad with a 3-1-1 record. In 2002, he also led the PGA Tour in rounds in the 60s, with 56.

WENDY WARD
Wendy Ward, a *Golf Digest* Playing Editor, has won three times since joining the LPGA Tour in 1996. The 1994 U.S. Women's Amateur champion, Ward has competed in two Solheim Cup competitions.

FOREWORD

You can have all the pretty scenery, the communing with nature, the long walks with old friends. But when all is said and done, the one thing that really gets you going on the golf course is the last number you write on your scorecard. The other stuff is great, but be honest, the first thing you want to know is, "What'd I shoot?" And right after that it's usually, "If I'd only done such-and-such, then I'd have broken 100 (or 90 or 80)."

The game of golf is a social one, sure, but it's also a game of private achievements and personal break-throughs. Ask a golfer the date of his anniversary and he might have to think about it. Ask him the date he broke 100 and chances are he'll name the course, describe the weather, list his playing partners and recount his best shots of the round—every single one of them.

While golfers laugh about their quixotic addiction to improvement, their amusement should not be confused with lack of commitment. Once the 100 barrier is hurdled, there is 90, 80, and, for the very best, 70. One golfer we know has based every one of his 15-plus electronic passwords on "68," the only score

he ever shot under 70. It happened 10 years ago. Like to know how he did it, shot by shot? Just ask him.

The pursuit of improvement drives golfers to the practice range, the putting green and to *Golf Digest's* most popular instruction feature, "Breaking 100, 90, 80." This monthly guide to the scoring basics speaks to the elemental desire of every golfer, from the new-comer to the veteran, to get the ball in the hole in as few as strokes as possible.

A magic word, "possible." For that's the true beauty of the game. At the start of each round, anything is possible—from your longest drive ever to the purest iron you've ever hit to your first hole-in-one. And, especially, your lowest score ever.

You think it's impossible to break your scoring barrier or that it would take the kind of commitment to honing skills and practicing drills that you don't want to make? No matter what you're shooting now, you already are capable of taking your game to the next level.

Try an experiment. Think about what you usually make on each hole at your home course (use fractions if you're between numbers). It's a good bet that when you add

up the average number of strokes for each hole, you get a score remarkably close to, if not already better than, your next scoring barrier.

Of course, you can't go from shooting 108 to 84 overnight. That sort of improvement takes more time and more work. However, to make the jump from a 90s shooter to an 80s shooter does not require a special diet, all-new equipment and six months of beating balls on the practice range. It's within your grasp right now. You need to understand that you don't have to become a different player to reach that new level.

It's very much like when a tour player who hasn't won finally goes out and wins a tournament. David Duval, who went almost three full years on tour before he won, ran off a stretch of eight victories in the 15 months following his first win. He said he just came to the realization that he didn't have to do anything extraordinary to win. All he had to do was go out and play his usual game.

A golfer's breakthroughs don't only occur on the scorecard. They come in every aspect of the game. "I finally hit a drive over the hill on No. 1," you'll hear a buddy say. Or, "Do you realize that's the first time I ever got up and down from that bunker?" Or, "Hey, I got on No. 4 in two. Wow!!!" In every area of the game, there are opportunities for personal bests. Some golfers approach things that way. Some have to learn. *Breaking 100, 90, 80* aims to help you raise your level of play off the tee, from the fairway, in the sand, around the green and close to the hole. We promise breakthroughs in every part of your game, and that, of course, will lead to scoring breakthroughs at the end of your round.

Guaranteed.

Chapter 1

TEE SHOTS

*Players who score well
put their tee shots in play.
Hit more fairways
with a consistent,
repeatable swing and
smart driving strategy.*

TEE SHOTS

Hitting More Fairways

Getting safely off the tee is a prerequisite to scoring well. Hitting your drive in the fairway not only allows you to play your next shot from the optimal position, it also has a positive effect on your mental outlook and playing strategy. Consider the opposite scenario: A poor drive can have a ripple effect on your game that forces you into recovery mode. The result is likely at least one dropped shot per each fairway missed for most players.

The good news is that your tee shot is the one full-swing shot you take from an ideal position—from a stance of your own choosing, your ball sitting on a tee. Make the most of this opportunity with the right strategy, preshot routine and swing thought.

Your choice of driving club is crucial. While today's supersize drivers are longer and more forgiving than ever, they may not be the most accurate club—or even the longest off the tee—for you. Choose the club that will allow you to swing freely, for distance and, more important, for accuracy.

Previous spread: Tiger Woods off the tee demonstrates a perfect blend of power and control.

Rising PGA Tour star Aaron Baddeley makes solid contact off the tee.

How to Hit More Fairways Without Changing Your Swing

AIM TO ONE SIDE

Everybody has a natural ball-flight tendency. Some hit the ball right to left; most go left to right. It doesn't matter what you do, as long as you allow for it. If you often slice your tee shots, tee up on the right side of the tee box, aim down the left side of the hole and let the ball curve into play.

Randy Smith on alignment.

STEER CLEAR OF HAZARDS OFF THE TEE

If there's trouble to the right of the fairway, tee up on the right side of the tee box. Trouble left? Tee it up on the left side. That gives you the best angle to hit away from any hazards.

NARROW YOUR FOCUS

Smaller, precise targets make for smaller misses. The next time you see a wide fairway, narrow your focus and imagine it's the tightest fairway in the U.S. Open. Pick one small spot on the fairway and try to hit it with your tee shot. Even if you don't often hit that exact spot, none of your misses will stray far from the intended target.

Janet Coles on visualization.

The Big Obstacles to Getting Off the Tee? A Poor Grip and Poor Posture

HOLD THE CLUB MORE IN THE FINGERS, NOT IN THE PALM

Work on forming and re-forming your grip at every opportunity—even at home sitting in front of the TV. Right-handed players should start with the left hand. Hold the club so it runs diagonally from the base of the little finger to the crook of the forefinger. Don't hold the club in the palm. The in-palm position may feel more secure at first, but it actually creates tension and reduces mobility of the wrist. With your left hand, raise the club in front of you with the toe up. You should see two or three knuckles of the left hand and a distinct "cupping" of the left wrist. Feel how the last three fingers support the weight of the club? That's the key to being able to hinge the wrists correctly.

KEEP YOUR SPINE ANGLE CONSTANT

If you can return the club to the ball in almost the same position as you were in at address, you will have maintained your spine angle and should make good contact. Don't straighten up your body or right leg during the transition from the backswing to the downswing. Keep some flex in your right knee as you shift your weight onto the left side through impact. Think about keeping the same angles all the way through your swing.

Jane Crafter on posture.

SPRING INTO ACTION

At setup, you need to be in an athletic position to make good contact. Bend from the hips, not the back, and avoid hunching your shoulders. Your weight should be balanced on the balls of your feet, rather than back on your heels. Have some bend in your knees. Be like a diver ready to take off.

How to Make More Consistent Contact Off the Tee

YES

Hank Haney on swing plane.

SWING MORE AROUND YOUR BODY THAN UP-AND-DOWN

To break 100, you have to avoid the disasters: fat shots, topped shots, popped-up drives. To hit the ball squarely with your irons, the clubhead has to travel at a slight downward angle. With your woods, particularly tee shots, the clubhead approaches the ball at a more level, or even slightly upward, angle. An extreme downward angle—a steep swing like that shown below—makes solid contact difficult. Know that the basic shape of the swing isn't up and down. It's more around your body, like that shown at left. This is true for the irons, and even more true for your woods, which have longer shafts that require you to shallow out your swing.

NO

NO

SHIFT YOUR WEIGHT AS YOU SWING BACK

In a reverse pivot, the weight remains on the front side in the backswing. From here, solid, consistent contact is very difficult. A good body motion involves starting centered over the ball and turning your upper body away from the ball as your lower body resists. When you do this correctly, you should feel tension along the inside of your right leg as your weight shifts. How do you know you're doing it right? At the top, you should feel as if you can't hold the position for more than a couple of seconds.

NO MORE 'FROSTY' SCORES

Getting your game consistently into the 90s means eliminating from your scorecard all the numbers that have names: the snowmen, the Bo Dereks, trips and quads.

YES

Putting It All Together to Start Every Hole the Right Way

LOFTED WOODS MAKE IT EASIER

Nothing ruins your score quicker than out-of-play
tee shots. Instead of risking a big number with an unreliable
driver, try a lofted fairway wood. Your shots will get in the air
easier and fly straighter. A fairway wood off the tee inspires
confidence—and it looks easy to hit, too. Your mis-hits won't
curve as much, so you'll stay in play.

FOR SOLID CONTACT, KEEP YOUR SWING UNDER CONTROL

Resist the urge to kill the ball. Tee it up so about half the ball
is above the clubface and just inside your left heel. Now
make a smooth, rhythmic swing at about 75 percent of your
maximum speed. Feel as if you've got too much club in your
hands. A three-quarter swing—the clubshaft not quite
horizontal at the top of the backswing—gives you all the
power you need, as long as you make a full shoulder turn.
Swinging under control means you'll be more likely to stay
behind the ball at impact, finish in balance and—most
important—hit the fairway.

Butch Harmon on rhythm.

Be Honest With Yourself: How Well Do You Hit That Big Driver?

THE SAD TRUTH ABOUT YOUR DRIVER

In a study of 1,200 golfers, not one player with a handicap of 14 or higher could hit a driver in the fairway 50 percent of the time. Each time you miss the fairway, figure it will cost you at least one stroke. That's too many shots to be giving up more than half the time.

A 3-WOOD CAN BE A POWERFUL DRIVER

The more comfortable you are over a shot, the better your chances of executing it successfully. Off the tee, the most comfortable club for the 100-shooter is the 3-wood. A 3-wood is easier to get airborne and has more backspin and less sidespin than a driver, which means it will slice or hook less. It has a shorter shaft than the typical driver and is heavier. A heavier club will give you more power if you don't generate a lot of clubhead speed.

Chuck Cook on club selection.

"BOWL" YOUR DRIVES

When aiming, try choosing a target you could bowl your ball toward. Unless there is no other choice, never aim over water, trees or bunkers. Knowing that you can mis-hit a shot (fat, thin, top, etc.) and still have it land safely will increase your confidence and, in turn, will improve your execution.

THE MENTAL SIDE

BOB ROTELLA VS. THE BIG STICK

A lot of people say they'd like to break 100, but if you watched them play, you'd probably say, "Your goal can't be to break 100, because you're hitting your driver off every tee and you haven't hit a fairway yet. So your *real* goal must be to hit driver on every hole." You can't strategize based on having a dream day with your most difficult club. Be honest. You've probably never even had a practice session where you've hit 14 good drivers in a row. Why all of a sudden are you going to do it today on the golf course? So keep practicing with the driver, but take a lofted wood or iron off the tee and start each hole in the fairway. You'll score lower—*that's* your goal.

Try Anything That Lets You See, Imitate and Feel Good Positions

Johnny Miller on practicing.

SEE WHAT IT FEELS LIKE

Videotape technology offers a perfect way to get visual feedback about your swing. Many pros and golf schools have video systems like the one shown here that offer an instant look at your swing and allow you to compare it to the swings of better players. But even a regular camcorder or mirror can be a revelation if you've never seen your swing. If you're trying to break 100, you should pay particular attention to your setup: grip, ball position, spine angle, knee flex and the alignment of your feet, knees, hips and shoulders. In the actual swing, make sure you're maintaining your set-up posture. Focus on the feel of swings that look good.

HIT BALLS INTO THE SETTING SUN

If you're a relatively poor ball-striker, you probably tend to be preoccupied with the outcome of the shot. That leads to tension, especially in the grip. Here's a solution: When you practice, hit balls into the setting (or rising) sun. Because it's difficult to see where the ball is going and you get amazing feedback about your swing and the quality of contact with the ball, you won't worry so much about the result. You'll lighten your grip pressure and hit the ball solidly.

TURN SCORING BREAKTHROUGHS INTO LONG-LASTING IMPROVEMENT

Some people define "breakthrough" as that one magical day when you play over your head and shatter your personal scoring barrier. But a genuine breakthrough occurs only when you start making that kind of special round an everyday occurrence. Of course, to achieve such long-lasting improvement you'll need help from a qualified PGA teaching professional.

When you sign up for lessons, just remember that the instructor is as determined to see you improve as you are. And although the instructor should be in control once the lessons begin, it never hurts to give a bit of direction beforehand. If you're a middle- or high-handicap player, ask the instructor to concentrate on the preswing fundamentals. Make sure the focus is on your grip, posture, alignment and ball position.

Alignment is especially important. Lay clubs parallel to each other on the ground as the golfer has done in the photo here. Hitting golf shots is a lot like shooting a gun—you must aim correctly if you intend to hit your target.

The bottom line is that improving is a systematic process. Start with the basics and you'll be surprised at how quickly you improve.

David Toms Swing Sequence: Staying in Rhythm

SWING YOUR ARMS AND BODY IN UNISON

You hear a lot of good players these days talk about keeping the club "in front" of them. What that means is that the player is trying to make a nice, smooth turn in the backswing that allows the arms to remain in front of the chest for as long as possible. In other words, the body, arms and hands work in unison.

David's swing is a great example of this, says his teacher Rob Akins (*below*). When he does it correctly, all he has to do on the downswing to produce an accurate shot is rotate his hips back toward the target until they are perpendicular to it. When his hips turn, the arms, hands and club simply come along for the ride. He no longer has to worry about manipulating the clubhead just before impact to make sure it's square to the target.

Some people call his a "body swing," since it's his shoulders in the backswing and hips in the follow-through doing all the work. You could also call it a rhythmic swing. His hands and arms stay in rhythm with his body. His tempo has become so good, he can work the ball left or right by making simple adjustments to his alignment and grip.

David Toms and swing coach Rob Akins.

Straight Talk for Slicers: Going Low Requires a Better Ball Flight

THE SHORTEST WAY BETWEEN TWO POINTS IS A STRAIGHT LINE

Train your mind, as well as your swing, to hit dead-straight shots. Imagine you have to drive it down a corridor of trees like the Avenue of the Oaks at Sea Island, Ga. You might feel as if you have to bunt it, but challenge yourself to swing harder while maintaining that same controlled motion.

Scott Davenport on visualization.

REDUCE YOUR SLICE WITH THE CORRECT BALL POSITION

To make solid contact with your driver, play the ball off your left heel. If you play the ball too far back in your stance, you will tend to chop down at it and lose distance or come over the top with an outside-to-in swing, usually causing a low pull or pop-up slice.

KEEP YOUR BALANCE

Imitate other athletes' "ready" positions. Keep your weight between the backs of your heels and the balls of your feet, which lets you pivot and turn.

For Solid Contact, Learn to Square Up Your Clubface at Impact

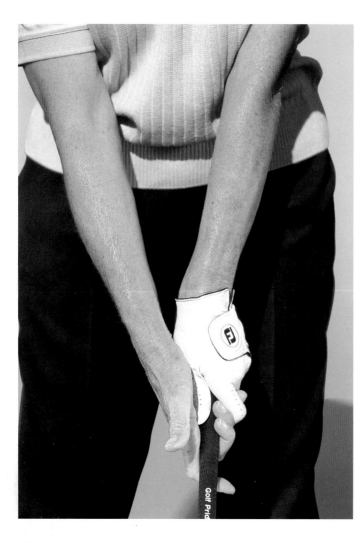

SWING A HOCKEY STICK TO CHECK YOUR FACE ANGLE

Sometimes it's hard to see what the clubface does during the swing. Use a hockey stick's large blade to help. Grip the stick as you would your golf club, then swing from hip high to hip high. Check your hands. If your left is in good position at impact—the back flat and facing the target—the blade should be square too.

Mark Winkley on clubface position.

SEE THREE KNUCKLES FOR STRAIGHTER, MORE POWERFUL SHOTS

Grip it so you can see three knuckles on your left hand. It'll be easier to keep the clubface square at impact and deliver some power to the ball. It also makes it easier to cock your wrists correctly and set the club at the top of the backswing. The grip itself can be overlapping, interlocking or "10-finger."

CURING YOUR SLICE STARTS WITH THE PROPER SETUP

The address position in the picture below is a typical slicer's setup. With a weak grip—which promotes an open clubface—the shoulders are aimed left of the target, and the hands are set behind the ball. From here, the slicer swings on a steep plane that makes the club swipe across the ball, as shown in the right photo. As a result, the ball will curve weakly to the right, robbing you of distance and accuracy.

Solve a lot of the slicer's swing problems before you even start your backswing:
- Set your feet and shoulders parallel to the target line;
- Tilt your spine slightly to the right, which will help allow the club to approach from a more inside-to-out path on the downswing;
- Position your hands slightly in front of the ball at address.

This setup will allow you to pivot your upper body over your lower body on the backswing, creating coil. The club can now approach on a shallower plane on the downswing, which translates into more consistent contact.

SLICE SWING

Don Hurter on the slice.

SLICE SETUP

Straighten Your Ball Flight by Working on These Anti-Slice Drills

PRACTICE DRILLS

Josh Zander on swing path.

HOW TO GROOVE AN IN-TO-OUT SWING PATH

Many golfers, slicers included, hear that a good swing comes from the inside. Mistakenly, they take the club back to the inside, starting a chain reaction that results in an over-the-top downswing. Coming over-the-top—the clubhead traveling from outside the target line to inside—results in a glancing blow at impact. If the clubface is closed, you'll hit a pull to the left. If it's square to the target line at impact, the ball will start straight but then fade to the right. If it's open, you'll hit a weak, pop-up even farther right.

To help take the club back on the target line, place one range ball about a foot behind the ball you're hitting. On the same line, four inches toward you, place another ball. Take the club back over the first ball, then swing through over the second.

WATCH YOUR WRIST

Another good anti-slice drill is to wear a wristwatch on the inside of your wrist. You should see the face on your follow-through.

USE YOUR ARMS TO HELP HOOK THE BALL

The easiest way to turn a slice swing into a draw swing is to focus on the position of your left forearm through impact. Using a middle iron and playing the ball off the ground (to better simulate on-course conditions), swing the club so your left forearm "rolls under" through impact. You want the right forearm to brush against the left as the club extends past impact. Your arms should be moving faster than your body on the downswing and the clubface should be rotating to a closed position at impact.

Janet Coles on drawing the ball.

Trade in Your Left-to-Right Ball Flight for a Right-to-Left Draw

START YOUR DRAW IN THE BACKSWING

Too many amateurs try to hook the ball by flipping their hands at impact. Instead, start your takeaway feeling as if the clubface is a little closed, with the clubhead going straight back rather than rolling open. This keeps the hands passive and sets up the proper inside move on the downswing.

GO FROM CLOSED TO OPEN

The clubface that felt closed on the backswing should feel as if it's opened up as it moves down to the ball. Don't roll the hands over at impact, either. Keep that right elbow tucked and swing out to the right. The clubhead sort of traces a loop, and the club almost feels like a whip coiling and then cracking just at impact.

Scott Davenport on hitting a draw.

TEST THE LONG AND SHORT OF IT

Many amateurs know how to find a club with the right shaft flex. But I'll bet nine out of 10 could not tell me the length of their driver. Trying to sell distance, most manufacturers have lengthened their clubs.

But the longer the club, the harder it is to control. Once, 43 inches was a standard driver length. Now it's closer to 45. When you buy clubs, try shorter shaft lengths. You may lose a few yards (or you may gain some, thanks to more-solid hits!), but you'll be in the fairway more often.

Charles Howell III's accuracy and power stem from a fluid, efficient blending of body rotation and arm swing. This synchronization is what produces torque, leverage and consistent contact.

You've Got Enough Game to Keep Your Swing in Sync. Here's How...

USE A MIRROR TO MAKE CHANGES

Many a golfer has learned to play by laying a *Golf Digest* flat on the ground, copying the positions they saw in it and checking them in a mirror. Using a mirror is a great learning tool, particularly to make adjustment in your setup. If you face the mirror, you can check your ball position—something even pros have to monitor constantly. From the side, you can check posture (*photo, right*) spine straight but tilted, arms hanging freely and knees slightly flexed.

IGNORE FREE ADVICE

Golfers are gullible. If we're not hitting the ball well, we'll listen to anybody's advice. But don't listen to your friends, unless they have a great knowledge of the golf swing. They're probably going to tell you something that has nothing to do with your real problem.

Rick Smith on the setup.

DON'T PRACTICE TIRED

Rehearsal swings on the range—where you don't hit the ball—can help, but don't overdo it. If you get tired, stop, even if you haven't used up all the balls you paid for or haven't fixed that day's swing problems. Tired swings create bad habits.

USE TRAINING AIDS TO KEEP YOUR SWING ON TRACK

Diagnose your own swing problems, then use training aids recommended by your swing coach to implement the necessary changes. Check to see if your clubface is square at the top of the backswing. The leading edge should be at a 45-degree angle to the ground. Another checkpoint: Your clubface is square at the top if the left wrist is flat and is at the same angle as an on-plane clubface.

You've Got a Swing You Can Trust. Now It's Time to Talk Strategy

CHOOSE THE SHOT

At this level, your thought process is much more important for lower scores than your technique. Your swing is solid, so use your ability to put the ball in play off the tee as an asset, not a liability. What you do before you swing is just as important as the actual swing motion.

Use your head to play to your strengths and away from your weaknesses. In this case, you want to hit a fade to hit it away from the water. Visualize the shot before you hit it. Make visualization part of your preshot routine.

STRETCH TO GET LOOSE

Develop a stretching routine that loosens all of your major muscle groups. Don't just rely on swinging a heavy club or a couple of irons.

John Elliott Jr. on preshot routine.

IMAGINE THE FIRST HOLE

Before you leave the range to start a round, "play" the first hole a few times—that is, actually go through your preshot routine and hit the kind of drive you want to hit on the first tee. Then go through your routine again and hit the kind of approach shot you'll have after your drive. You might even play the second hole this way, too. Tiger Woods finishes every pre-round warm-up on the range by hitting the shots he'll have on the first hole. That gives him confidence on the first tee.

HAVE A SINGLE KEY

You have thought about what you want to do. After a single rehearsal swing, forget about it. Focus on a single swing key or feel that will help you make a good motion and hit the ball solidly, the way you envisioned.

Use On-Course Practice Sessions to Ingrain the Value of Accurate Tee Shots

Peter Kostis on practice rounds.

PRACTICE YOUR WEAKNESSES

Average golfers, as a rule, are big on being realistic. One of the first rules of "game-improvement," regardless of your level of play, is to understand precisely where you are, not where you think you are. That way, instead of practicing just what you're good at, you'll spend some time working on those areas of your game that aren't so fun for you.

Instead of guessing, go out and really assess where you need help. There are two simple ways to do this:

First, play a 9-hole scramble with yourself, playing two balls. Play from the location of your best shot every time and see what your score is. Not only will this show you your potential, it will also give your self-confidence a little boost.

The second game is designed to reveal your weaknesses. Instead of playing the best ball, play the worst. If you manage to put both balls in the fairway but you can't hit the green with two tries, then your irons need some sharpening. If you hit two drives and both are in the boonies, then obviously you need to work on your driver (and you should probably start reaching for the 3-wood a little more).

HANG WITH THE BIG BOYS

Peer pressure can be a great motivator and teacher. One way to push yourself to lower scores is to play with better players. The match will be tighter, and you can learn just by watching them play.

Dean Reimuth on course management.

HOW IMPORTANT IS DRIVING ACCURACY? FIND OUT WITH THE 4-CLUB ROUND

No matter what your skill level, you can learn some important swing and course-management lessons by playing a round with four clubs—a 7-iron, a 5-iron, sand wedge and putter. Use the 5-iron for long shots, the 7-iron for approach shots and the sand wedge around the green. Use the same full swings for each club.

Notice how much easier the game is to play when you aren't hitting it sideways all day?

WHEN YOU TEE AN IRON

Tee the ball down low, like a perfect lie from the fairway. You'll compress the ball better and you'll be able to count on your normal trajectory and distance from whatever iron you use.

By Karrie Webb, LPGA Tour

MY FIRST TIME

◆ ◆ ◆

I'm not sure I can remember the first 18 holes of golf I ever played, but I can definitely remember the first 18 holes I played in competition. That was one round I'll never forget.

I was 8 years old, and it was a junior competition in Ayr, the small town where I grew up in Northern Queensland, Australia. I had just picked up the game—I don't think I had been playing six months at the time the tournament came around.

I shot 156 that day, and they gave me the Encouragement Award. Obviously, it meant "that was a good try, but you're a long way behind— keep practicing."

LPGA star Karrie Webb shot an "encouraging" 156 the first time she played 18 holes in competition. Since then, she's added a few more trophies, including the 2001 U.S. Women's Open.

Chapter 2

ACCURACY

*It's a game of how near,
not simply how far.
Here's how to dial in
distance and direction
with your irons.*

BREAKING 100 90 80

ACCURACY

Dialing in Distance and Direction

Making solid contact with your irons is fundamental to playing your best and achieving your scoring breakthroughs. First you must develop a repeatable swing that allows you to get the ball airborne and traveling toward your target on a consistent basis. Focus on your setup—grip, aim and alignment, posture and ball position. It's the foundation to any reliable swing.

Once you've mastered the basics, work on gaining control over distance and direction—the key to keeping the ball in play and hitting more greens. That means paying attention to ball flight. Any game-improvement plan must start with the question, "What is my ball doing?" Then work backward from there, diagnosing what your hands, arms and body are doing to affect the flight of the ball. Chances are your ball is curving too much, which reduces distance as well as directional control. Identify what is keeping your game from moving to the next level and improve it.

The goal for better players is to make better decisions on the course. For you, playing better golf isn't about making better swings as much as it is about making better choices. Even when you practice, get your mind totally focused on the target. Do that and your best-ever scores will follow.

Previous spread: Young Spanish superstar Sergio Garcia locks on his target.

Master teaching professional Chuck Cook proves that to make the ball go up, you must hit down on it, the key to crisp contact.

How to Hit More Greens With the Swing You've Got

PLAY 'THE BREAK' INTO THE GREEN

If you had a putt that sloped from left to right, you wouldn't aim straight at the hole. Then why aim for the flag when most of your shots curve to the right? Give yourself a better chance of hitting it at the target by aiming away from it.

Randy Smith on choosing your target.

TAKE MORE IRON ON APPROACH SHOTS

Make it a policy to always take an extra club when hitting into the green. Most 100-shooters are habitually short of the pin. Taking more club also encourages you to swing more smoothly.

Hank Haney on knowing your yardage.

LEARN YOUR DISTANCES

You can't hit greens if you have no idea of how far you hit your clubs. You can learn your distances at the range with just one club—the 6-iron, say. And you don't need to be that precise. Approximate the yardage using the marked flags. Hit 10 balls, ignore the shortest and the longest, and average the rest. Then add or subtract 10 yards for the next club.

Boost Consistency by Keeping Your Posture the Same With Every Swing

SHORE UP THE FOUNDATION TO YOUR SWING

The shape of both your backswing and your forward swing is greatly influenced by your posture. Having the proper foundation of good posture allows you to become more target-aware and less concerned with swing mechanics.

Your posture can disintegrate without you even knowing it. A change in body size—if you've lost or gained a few pounds—a kink in the back or a twinge in the knee can do it. To get your posture right, lay a club across your hips. Check to see that you are bending at the hips (*right*), not at the waist. And don't just squat with your knees (*below*). To complete your set-up position, just bend your knees slightly while tilted forward.

YES

NO

Jane Frost on posture.

SWING IN SLOW MOTION

When you practice a swing change, swing in slow motion, so you can feel the correct swing positions. You may also be amazed at how far you hit the ball when you swing slowly.

KEEP YOUR WEIGHT TOWARD THE BALLS OF YOUR FEET

When golfers are told to set up as if they were sitting, they often misinterpret this and end up sitting back on their heels. You can't dance, walk—or play golf—with your weight back on your heels. To perform any activity that requires movement, your weight should be toward the balls of your feet. Feel as if you can tap your heels on the ground. It's an athletic, ready-to-move position. Correct posture and weight distribution makes your swing more fluid.

For Improved Accuracy, Learn to Control Your Short Irons

Hank Johnson on the three-quarter swing.

SWING 'SHOULDER TO SHOULDER'

Learn to play three-quarter shots with your short irons. Most players are hung up on how far they can hit the 9-iron, not how accurately or consistently. Use Tiger Woods as your model. Nothing has contributed to his success more than learning to hit less-than-full shots with his short irons. Swing your short irons so your hands go back about even with your shoulders, and finish the same way. You will start knocking pins down, the way Tiger does.

CAN YOU SCORE FROM 100 YARDS?

See that 100-yard plate? Make it your office, says Bob Rotella. From here, you should be able to get into the hole in no more than three shots. That means scoring around bogey on every hole—and *that* means breaking 100.

Of course, to do this, you have to check your ego at the first tee. Unless you have a 9-iron or wedge in your hands, lay up to the 100-yard marker, even if that means hitting only a 30- or 40-yard shot. If you can't play three-shot golf from here, go work on your wedge game first. Stick with that strategy until you can shoot around 90. Think this is silly? Well, only about as silly as shooting 93 instead of 106. Besides, the good work with your wedge that helped you break 100 will later help you break 90 and 80.

Teach Yourself the Feel of a Solid Motion Through Impact

THE HEARTBEAT OF THE SWING

One of my favorite basic drills is to simulate the impact position at address, as I'm doing at left. With a 6- or 7-iron, my hands are slightly forward of the ball, which is positioned in the middle of my stance. My weight is turned to my left foot, my head is back and my right heel is off the ground. From there, I take a mini-swing and try to punch the ball, concentrating on solid impact. With this drill, you improve your swing arc and learn to make good contact. It also helps you build a real feel for the position you need to get into to make solid contact.

Rick Smith on solid contact.

Todd Anderson on swing shape.

USE A MINI-SWING TO CHECK YOUR SHAFT ANGLE

There are ideal angles for the clubshaft to be in as you swing. If your angles are inconsistent, you'll make inconsistent contact and start the ball off-line. To hit a straight shot, the shaft should point just inside the ball-target line throughout the swing. Use a three-quarter swing to check (*above*). Swing to a three-quarter follow-through, keeping the same position. Make this mini-swing to feel the correct swing shape and clubface rotation, with the shaft angles matching on both sides of the ball.

Working on a Swing Change? Then Keep Your Practice Sessions Simple

PRACTICE DRILLS

USE AN IRON OFF A TEE

When you're working on a swing change, make things as simple as possible on the practice range. Use a 7-iron or 8-iron and tee the ball to make it easier to get it in the air. Remember: You shouldn't focus on how far the ball goes, only on the swing positions you're trying to find. Don't clutter your mind with too many swing thoughts, only the one thing you're working on.

CHECK YOUR AIM

With every shot you hit on the practice range, you should have a target. Hit a ball to a target on the right side of the range, then a ball on the left side of the range. This forces you to concentrate on your aim, your alignment and your set-up routine before each shot, so you won't get sloppy. If you lay clubs on the ground to help your alignment (*below*), place one club near the ball pointing at the target and the other parallel to it behind your heels.

Butch Harmon on how to practice.

The secret to Annika Sorenstam's
success? In a word, accuracy.
She hits nearly eight out of 10
fairways and greens in regulation
per round. With that kind of control,
low scores are sure to follow.

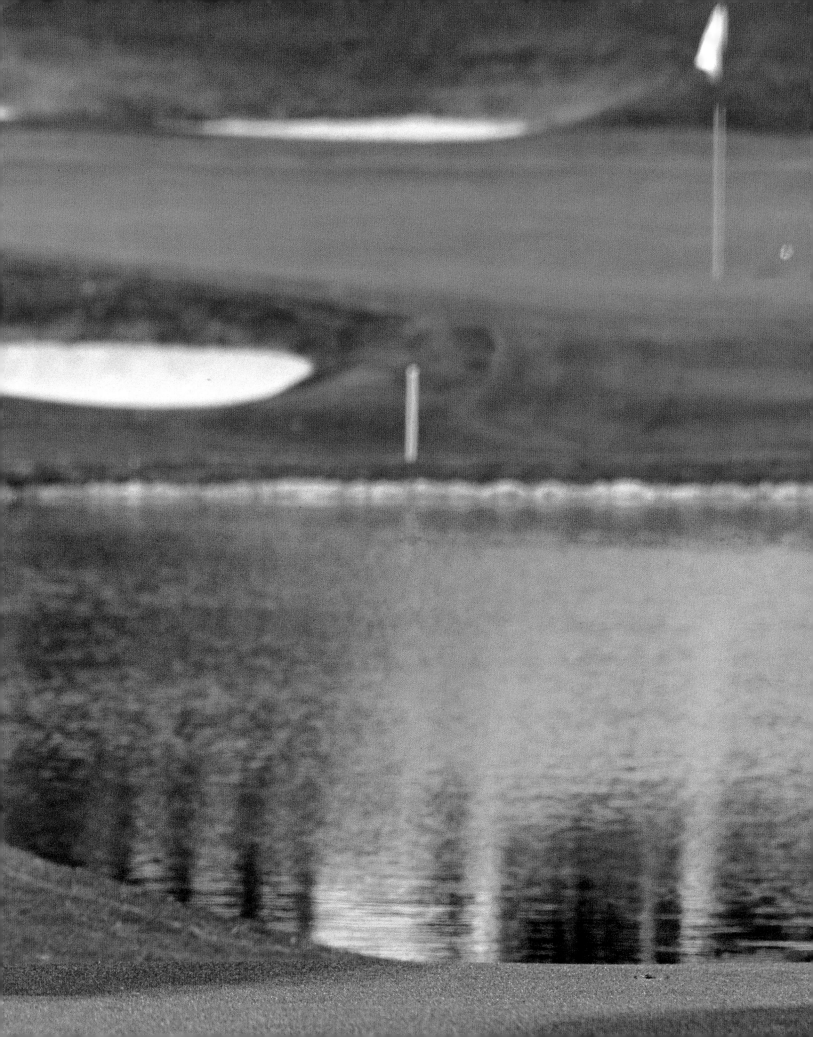

For More Consistent Ball-Striking, Improve Your Impact Position

LEARN TO TRAIN YOUR HANDS

This is a great drill to cure hitting from the top—releasing the club too early. Draw a line in the sand of a fairway bunker about two inches behind your left heel, as in the small photo below. With full swings, try to make divots on the target side of the line, as I'm doing in the large photo. Be sure the divot aims at the target. When you can do that consistently, you've educated your hands for consistent ball-club contact.

Mark Winkley on solid contact.

PAINT THE DIVOT ON IRON SHOTS

To hit crisp iron shots, the club strikes the ball first and then the ground. This means the divot should start at the impact position and continue ahead of it. To get a feel for this, imagine there is a paint brush on the end of a golf shaft. Now think of painting a divot with the brush starting at the impact position and moving toward the target. To paint it, your hands have to stay in front of the brush past impact and drag it through.

WHEN YOU TEE AN IRON

Tee the ball down low, like a perfect lie from the fairway. You'll compress the ball better and you'll be able to count on your normal trajectory and distance from whatever iron you use. No matter how good they are, most players should use a tee any time it's allowed. That includes par 3s where you need only an 8- or 9-iron. It's the only chance you have to guarantee a good lie. Take it.

Focus on the Left Hand to Hit Crisp, Accurate Irons

KEEP THAT LEFT WRIST FIRM—JUST LIKE LEE

The biggest mistake made by poor players, medium players and experts—and it runs from the full swing to the chip shot to the putt—is the breaking down of the left wrist through impact.

The only things the left wrist and hand must do in the golf swing are hang on to the club and not break down. Collapsing the left wrist on the full swing causes an instant loss of power and accuracy.

The poor player is prone to slap at the ball, jerk back from it, actually quit on the shot in an effort to help the ball in the air. The way to get the ball into the air with some authority is to swing down and through with a firm left wrist. Watch Lee Trevino here. He looks as if he hits the ball with the back of his left hand.

THE LEFT HAND CONTROLS CLUBFACE POSITION

Any movement in the left hand directly influences clubface position. If you've started with the correct grip, the back of the left hand should be flat and face the target at impact. To experience this sweet feeling, swing at an impact bag or similar object. You'll square the clubface and use the entire club in the swing, not just the clubhead.

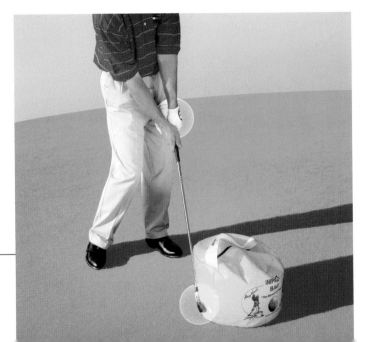

ADJUST YOUR GRIP FOR CURVES

For your grip, make adjustments that counteract the way you curve the ball. If you slice, turn both of your hands to the right on the grip. If you hook, turn them to the left.

VERTICAL HANDS MEAN A SQUARE FACE

When your hands are below your belt in the swing, they should be perpendicular to the ground, which translates into a square clubface. That's a tough thing to check with a club, but an easy thing to see if you hold a Ping Pong paddle in each hand. Start your backswing, but stop at waist level (*right*). Both paddles should be straight up and down. Then swing through to a waist-high position after the ball, as in the photo below. Again the paddles are perpendicular.

Tom Ness on clubface position.

As Ball-Striking Great Ben Hogan Once Said, 'The Secret Is in the Dirt'

DIAGNOSE YOUR DIVOTS

One way to give real direction to your practice is to scrape a line in the grass on the tee, perpendicular to your target line, as Randy Smith is doing here. Then place a row of balls directly on the line and hit them.

If you're hitting your irons correctly, all the divots will be thin scrapes of turf that start just after the line and point directly at your target. If a divot starts before the line (like the top divot below), you're hitting too far behind the ball. No divot at all means you're either topping it or not hitting with enough of a downward blow. If your divot is pointing to the left, you're cutting across the ball from outside to in, with a slice the likely result.

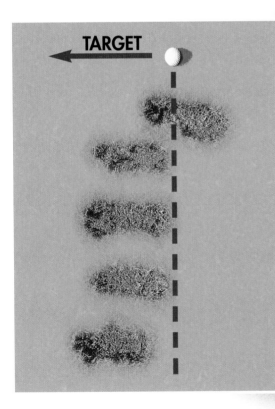

TARGET

DRIVE THE TEE FOR CRISP SHOTS

Use this drill to groove a feeling about where the divot should be on a standard middle- or short-iron shot: Stick a tee into the ground on an angle, so that the top of it rests just behind the target side of the ball (*right*). Hit some three-quarter shots and try to drive the tee into the ground (*below*). This is a perfect way to focus your practice at the range.

DON'T BE A SODBUSTER

If you are creating giant-size King Kong divots, you're digging too deeply into the ground. What you want to do is nip the the turf and create a shallow divot as you swing through the shot.

Your Swing Doesn't Stop at Impact—Finish It for Longer, Stronger Shots

HOLD YOUR FINISH FOR THREE SECONDS

Your goal is to apply even force through the top of the backswing through to the finish. You shouldn't be trying to speed up the clubhead at any point. The best way to get a feel for this idea is to concentrate completely on the finish position of your hands. Hit some practice shots at the range, and hold your finish for three full seconds. Try to keep the pressure in your hands equal from start to finish. You'll be less impact-oriented, and your balance will improve as well.

THE GOLDEN SPIKE AWARD

Get most of your weight onto your left side in the follow-through, so a person behind you can see every spike on the bottom of your right shoe.

KNOW YOUR DISTANCES

If you can play an empty course, buy a yardage book or a laser distance finder and chart the exact distance you hit each club. It will clarify your club decisions later.

THE GREEN IS A LARGE TARGET

The average green is 30 to 36 yards deep. The average player has a 10- to 12-yard differential between irons. That means you can hit three different clubs to the green. Yet most players pick the shortest, making hitting the green impossible with less-than-perfect contact. Moral: Know how far you hit each club, and use one club more than you think—all the time.

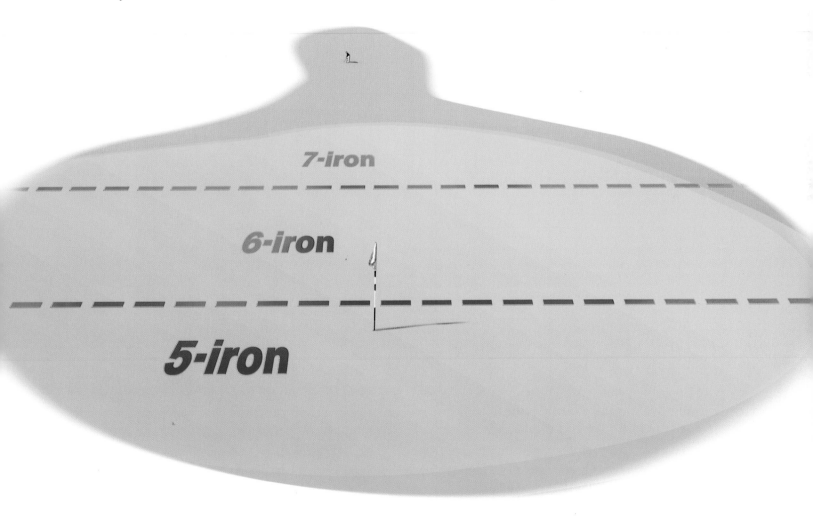

7-iron

6-iron

5-iron

Easy Steps to Gain More Control Over Your Ball Flight

FADE

Brewster Bassett on alignment.

DRAW

LET YOUR EYE-LINE DETERMINE YOUR SHOT SHAPE

One of the simplest ways to improve a slicer's swing is to change his or her eye-line. Slicers tend to orient their eyes to the left (*above left*). This encourages an out-to-in slice swing. Simply by shifting their eye-line to the right (*above right*), many slicers will improve the alignment of their shoulders at address and swing

more in-to-out, straightening their ball flight or even hitting a draw.

Even if you don't slice, you can apply this same principle to working the ball, which can help you get to tight pins. When you want to hit a fade, align your eyes left of the target. When you want to hit a draw, align your eyes to the right of the target. Keep the clubface aligned at the target itself.

HITTING SLICES? TRY OFFSET CLUBS

Many of the biggest-selling iron models are offset—i.e., the leading edge of the club is set slightly behind the shaft. With offset, your hands are more likely to be in front of the clubhead at impact, which is the position you have to be in to avoid a slice. In effect, this closes the clubface slightly and allows you to hit straight shots or draws. Offset clubs could improve your ball flight.

PRACTICE DRILLS

ALWAYS PRACTICE WITH A PURPOSE

Many players go to the range and just practice the things they already do well. Instead, you should focus on your weaknesses. A lot of golfers trying to break 90 have a hard time hitting long irons, for example. If that's you, spend most of your time hitting just long irons until you're comfortable with them. Also try working on opposites. For example, try hitting hooks—even duck hooks. Don't worry about how to do it—just try to do it. Often your body will find a way to do it instinctively.

Hank Haney on smart practice.

HIT PRACTICE SHOTS FROM ONE EDGE OF THE RANGE

Many players have misconceptions about how they hit the ball on the range, because the wide open space there doesn't give them any frame of reference for a shot. On the course, a fairway or a green is a specific framing target. That's why I like to have my students hit balls from one side of the range, preferably the left—especially for slicers. The nets (or whatever barriers your have at your range) on

that side provide perspective for each shot. It's easier to see just how much you're fading or drawing it.

TAKE YOUR MULLIGANS DURING PRACTICE ROUNDS

To integrate the shots you practice into your real rounds, play by yourself early or late in the day and experiment a little. If you hit a bad one, drop another and try again.

Nick Price Swing Sequence: Mastering the Short Irons

FOCUS ON THE FUNDAMENTALS
TO BUILD A SMOOTH, FLUID SWING

The golf swing is all about motion. No matter what the dynamics are, no matter what kind of positions you're in during the swing, when you have a fluid motion, you can play this game. So I always try to swing smooth through the ball.

What I like the most about swinging the 9-iron is that it's a great club to build the foundation for your golf swing. You can really groove your swing by hitting a lot of short irons and then copying those positions with every club.

One thing that is very important is to complete the backswing. The tendency for amateurs is to swing a little quicker with their short irons. They make a poor transition from the backswing to the downswing. I try not to get quick. I want the same smooth motion with a 9-iron as I would with any other shot.

I can't stress enough the importance of developing a routine and sticking with it. Don't jump from one swing theory to another. I am constantly working on the fundamentals of the golf swing. I won't make a radical change, rather, I try to hone the important aspects of the swing. I constantly check my grip, my posture and alignment. Do the same during your practice sessions and you'll have much better success with your scoring clubs.

Nick Price shares his short-iron secrets.

Learn 'The Body Swing'—The Pro-Style Move for Added Control

TURN THE BODY MORE, RELEASE THE HANDS LESS

For a controlled swing, make a punch-shot motion with a shorter backswing and more body turn on the downswing. The arms and body should move through the ball as a unit. Focus on the body rotation to the target and the hands finishing high with no release (*right*). Avoid a flippy release where the right hand crosses over the left on the follow-through (*below*).

YES

NO

Scott Davenport on the "no-hands" swing.

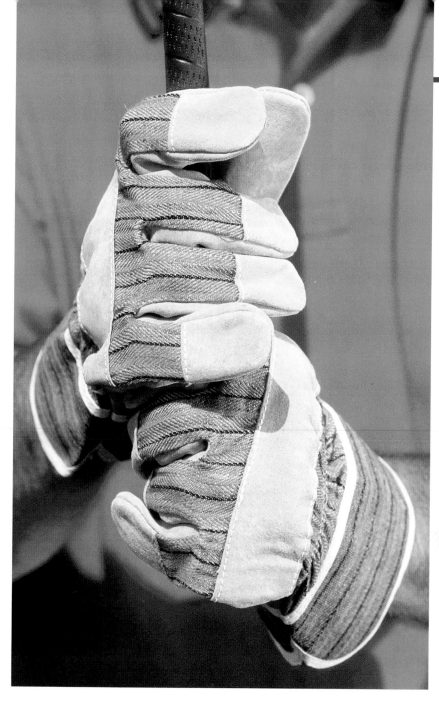

PUT THE GLOVES ON
TO TAKE THE HANDS OUT

Here's an unusual, but very effective, practice drill from Rick Smith: Hit some balls with heavy work gloves on. It really helps you make sure you are swinging the club on the proper path and not manipulating the clubhead to get it in position at impact. If you hit solid shots with the gloves on, you'll know your path is good. If it's just impossible, you'll know your hands are doing too much work. Let your hands just come along for the ride.

CHOOSE A BALL, THEN COMMIT

Test a variety of golf balls and find the one that gives you the best blend of distance (generally the result of a firmer cover or core compression) and control (higher spin rate due to a softer cover or lower compression). But whichever one you choose, stay with that model. That way, you'll always know what distance you can hit each shot.

How to Keep the Club On-Plane Coming Down

DON'T LET THE CLUB GET STUCK BEHIND YOU

Some better players go overboard in their effort to produce a draw by exaggerating the inside-to-out move. If you do this, your club "gets stuck" behind your body on the downswing. That forces you to manipulate your hands to square the face. If you've got great timing and an unlimited practice schedule, you can play this way.

Otherwise, you'll be doomed to inconsistent ball-striking. An on-plane downswing returns the club at the same angle as the backswing. In the photo on the right, you can see the difference. The shaft bisects the angle created by my right and left forearms. I don't have to use my hands to square the face at all, and can just release the club toward the target. Get on-plane and your accuracy and consistency will instantly improve.

Hank Haney on getting on-plane.

NO

YES

BACKSWING

DOWNSWING

David Leadbetter on swing path.

USE THE 8 O'CLOCK DRILL TO GET 'UNSTUCK'

To improve your downswing position, picture your body as a clock face. At the 8 o'clock position going back (*left*), the clubhead should be closer to the target line than the club handle is. The ideal position for the club at the 8 o'clock position on the downswing is nearly identical. That pre-impact position is really important, because where the club is at 8 o'clock determines where the club is at impact. Practice working the club down to an 8 o'clock position in which the clubhead is outside the handle. Nick Price often uses this drill.

by Justin Leonard, PGA Tour

MY FIRST TIME

♦ ♦ ♦

I've always been goal-oriented. By the time I was 12, I had never broken 80. A lot of times, I'd get to the 15th hole and I'd be 8 over par (par was 71). I'd think, "If I can just par in, I'll break 80." Then I'd make double on 16 and it would be, "Ooh, I can't believe I did that." Then I'd shoot 81.

One day, I played with two members at our club, Royal Oaks Country Club in Dallas, who I didn't really know. I didn't carry a scorecard with me. I just kept track in my head. I was 8 over on the 18th tee. It's a par 5. I hit a driver, second shot down the fairway, then hit the third shot on the front edge of the green. Then I two-putted for my par. It was pretty routine, but I knew that I had finally broken 80.

Afterward, I found a scorecard, wrote down my score for each hole and ran out to the parking lot to find the guys I had just played with to have them sign and attest it. Without any proof that I really did shoot 79, and had witnesses to it, my dad would be like, "Yeah, sure you did."

They looked at me kind of funny but said, "OK, sure," and signed my card. They probably would have signed it for a 69 if I had asked. I think they just wanted to get home.

Leonard grew up playing Royal Oaks C.C. with Harrison Frazar, who was his roommate at the University of Texas and who eventually joined him on the PGA Tour. Leonard continues to be involved with junior golf, serving as National Co-Chairman of the American Junior Golf Association.

Chapter 3

POWER

The engine that drives
every shot is a powerful
athletic motion. Here's how to
build a repetitive swing
to hit the ball farther.

POWER

Hitting the Ball Farther

Maximizing distance isn't everything in your quest for lower scores, but it sure helps. Once you've succeeded in gaining some control over the direction of your shots, it's time to unleash your power potential. If you can hit your full-swing shots farther, you'll gain more ground with every stroke. And that's a big part of getting the ball in the hole in as few as strokes possible.

The key to the long game is learning how to build a repetitive swing that enables you to strike the ball solidly and hit the ball straighter. It also means adding as much clubhead speed as possible while still swinging in control. After all, there's little sense in hitting the ball farther if it only results in sending it deeper into the woods or tall grass.

For players striving to break 90 and 80, the quest for more distance usually means learning to hit a draw, a ball flight that, for right-handed players, travels from right to left. When you hit a draw, the clubhead approaches the ball at a more powerful angle, producing a more penetrating ball flight. If the fairways are firm, count on a draw to give you more roll upon landing. Greater distance with the draw swing doesn't apply only to the driver. You'll be hitting 7-irons where you used to hit 5-irons.

Previous spread: 2002 PGA Champion Rich Beem bombs one off the tee.

The epitome of power on the PGA Tour, John Daly has won a record 11 driving-distance titles, averaging over 310 yards per drive in 2003.

Master the Basics of a Powerful Setup and Body Turn

GET IN POSITION BEHIND THE BALL

People who don't break 100 set up poorly with the driver. Typically, they position the ball toward the back of their stance and then chop down on it as if they're hitting a 5-iron. To set up correctly, first put the ball forward in your stance, in line with the left heel. Place 60 percent of your weight on your right foot. Your shoulders are square to the target, with the right shoulder lower than the left. You want to put your body in position to really "get behind" the ball on the backswing. On the downswing you'll be able to shift your weight forward, hitting the backside of the ball with a powerful, slightly upward blow.

YOUR HEAD STAYS BACK, TOO

Let your head move backward a bit in the backswing to accommodate the shifting of weight to the right foot as Tom Kite demonstrates below. Let it move even an extra bit backward during the downswing. The head must stay behind the ball. Moving the head forward during the downswing is a power killer.

David Leadbetter on ball position.

WIDEN YOUR STANCE FOR A SOLID BASE

When you're hitting your driver, widen your stance to hit the ball farther, placing your feet outside your shoulders. First, it helps you make an elongated takeaway and a wide backswing arc. Second, it restricts your hip action, helping you build coil. Third, it makes it easier to shift your weight to the left on the downswing. Fourth, it improves your balance. And fifth, it extends the flat spot of your swing through impact, ensuring powerful hits. Flaring out your right foot can also help you make a more powerful turn away from the ball.

YES

NO

For Maximum Distance, Don't Rush the First Move Down

PAUSE TO PACK POWER INTO YOUR SWING

Make sure that you complete your backswing—even to the point where you feel you have a slight pause at the top. Visually it won't look like there's any pause at all. But in your mind, you should feel as if there's a point that you are trying to get to before you start back down. Many golfers never get to that point, and start down before they're ready. As a result, their rhythm and positioning are out of whack. Complete your windup so that you feel a pause. Then you'll be in good shape to start the downswing smoothly and with power.

GET THE RIGHT FLEX

Many amateurs use golf shafts that are too stiff for their swing speed, says Scott Davenport. Most would be better off with a more flexible club, one with a regular or even senior shaft. The rule of thumb for shaft flex: If you hit it too high or too far (wouldn't that be great?) get a firmer shaft. Otherwise, forget about what Tiger Woods and other big hitters are using, and get a shaft with more flex.

WHEN TO TURN IT ON

To hit the ball farther, you must generate more club-head speed, at the proper time. You don't necessarily have to be strong to do this, but you have to be aggressive at certain points in the swing. This doesn't mean wildly flailing away at the ball. In fact, if you are too aggressive or quick at the top of your swing, you will not hit the ball farther. Instead, the generation of speed must be accompanied by a certain rhythm.

Start the swing with a smooth, although not necessarily slow, takeaway. Continue to think "smooth" as you change direction at the top of your swing, when the club goes from up to down. If you keep these two areas smooth and rhythmical, you can accelerate on the downswing as much as you want and go aggressively after the ball, as long as you stay in balance.

Judy Rankin on tempo.

Creating a Fluid Body Motion Through Impact

Todd Anderson on sychronization.

HANDS AND FEET MOVE IN RHYTHM

Remember that the club, hands and your arms aren't the only things moving back and forth during the swing. Your feet move, too, in rhythm with the hands, to help create smooth movements. To feel this, hold a milk crate or basket of balls with both hands and swing back and through to waist height. Start with the arms only, then let the feet move in tandem with the arms, the heels coming up slightly. This arms/feet movement mimics the actual golf swing.

SHAKE OUT YOUR HANDS

Golf is a social game. For you, the high-handicapper seeking to hit the ball as far as you can, that's a problem. The anxiety you experience playing in front of others usually translates into tight muscles that don't perform correctly. When you feel tense or afraid, blood doesn't flow as well to your limbs. Before you tee off, shake your arms and hands to increase circulation.

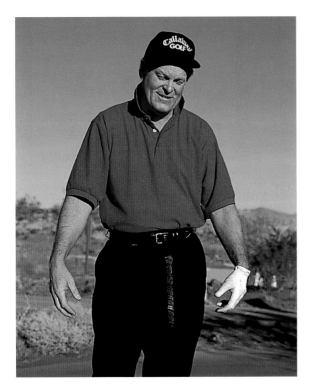

PLAY SMART: USE THE RIGHT SET OF TEES

If you think you'll impress a playing partner by hitting from the back tees before you're good enough, that'll only last until you struggle through the first few holes. For a fair test, play the tees that match your ability. It's more fun and saves time.

Johnny Miller on the finish.

GIVE YOURSELF A WHACK ON THE BACK

A great way to acquire a graceful, powerful downswing is to improve the quality of your follow-through. When you practice, concentrate on achieving such a full, free finish that you kiss yourself on the back with the clubshaft at the completion of the swing. For whatever reason, the freedom needed to do that transfers wonderfully into the downswing.

Ingrain the Proper Sequence of Motion to Produce a Powerful Swing

PRACTICE DRILLS

GET YOUR BODY MOTION IN ORDER GOING BACK...

A simple way to get the pieces of your swing in sync is to use a paper cup as an indicator. Poke a quarter-size hole in the bottom of the cup and slide it onto the shaft of your driver, mouth-side down. On the backswing, pause at the top to let the cup slide all the way down the shaft to your hands. Not only will this pause allow you to fully coil your shoulders, but it will keep you from making a violent transition from backswing to downswing—a major drain on power and a source of erratic play.

Dean Reinmuth on timing.

YES

NO   **NO**

...AND COMING DOWN THROUGH IMPACT

If you've sequenced your downswing correctly, the cup will slide down and click against the head of the driver right at impact. That way you're generating maximum speed and power. If you don't fully release the club, as in the left photo above, the cup will be sliding down the shaft after the clubhead passes the impact point.

Release the hands and wrists too early, as in the top right photo, and the cup will slide all the way down the shaft before the clubhead gets to the ball. Not only have you wasted power, but you can't do much more than hit an over-the-top pull or slice from there.

Eliminate the Power Leaks That Slow Down Your Swing

TENSION IS THE ENEMY

One of the keys to breaking the next scoring barrier is developing more clubhead speed. You won't do that with tight muscles. They need to be free and relaxed to generate speed in the swing. It all starts at address. The inset photo below shows the setup of a player who won't hit the ball very far. When you're that tense, there's no way you can make the full, fluid motion necessary for developing clubhead speed. You need to look more like the picture at left: arms and hands loose, body relaxed, chin up. This position makes a powerful swing possible.

Randy Smith on staying relaxed.

NO

SPEED AND DISTANCE

The lower your clubhead speed, the more distance you will gain with a more lofted club. Novice, women and senior golfers especially will hit it farther teeing off with a driving club with at least 15 degrees of loft.

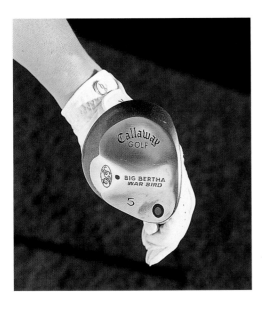

THINK 'OILY' WITH YOUR GRIP

A reminder: Use constant pressure and be like this oily robot, holding the club firmly, so the wrists can hinge and release freely. Too tight a grip creates seized-up joints.

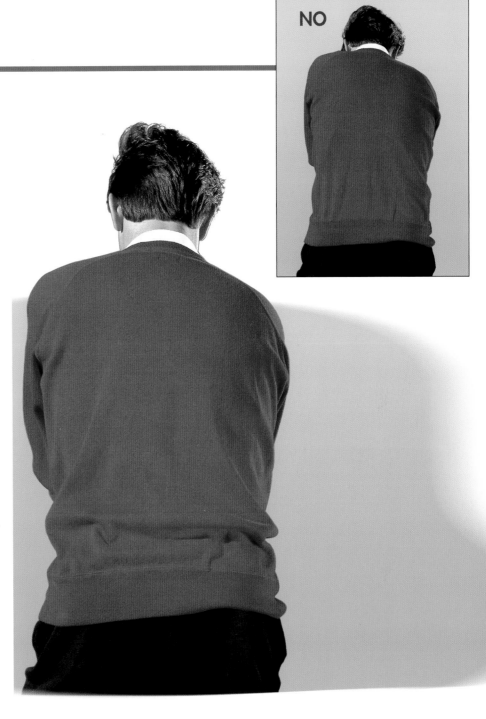

NO

PUT YOUR TENSION BEHIND YOU

Tension often manifests itself in how you hold the club—a death grip, with white knuckles and arms of steel—but it comes from the bigger muscles in your back. Ease the tension in your swing by loosening the area between the shoulder blades just under the neck. The looseness will trickle down to your shoulders, arms and hands. A relaxed address position will allow you to make a bigger, freer swing. The result: more clubhead speed and longer shots.

Get Longer With the Proper Hinging and Unhinging of Your Wrists

Peter Kostis on wrist action.

COCK YOUR WRISTS TO UNLEASH MORE POWER

There can be a lot of technical things to think about in the golf swing—too many things, frankly. But if you're trying to break 90, you need to keep it simple. So focus on this one key move: Hinge the wrists before your hands reach shoulder height on the backswing, unhinge the wrists on the downswing and then hinge them again before your hands reach shoulder height on the follow-through. Practice and play with this compact, effortless motion, even if that means "chipping" every shot until it becomes more natural. Master this move and you'll consistently deliver the front of the club to the back of the ball.

THE 'L' DRILL TEACHES HANDS AND ARMS

Stick a tee in the vent hole of your 8-iron grip, then swing the club back to a three-quarter position (*below left*). The shaft and your right forearm should form a 90-degree angle. Allow your body to turn as a result of your arm swing—no independent body coiling. From this position, swing the club briskly to a three-quarter finish (*below right*). Again, the shaft and your left forearm form a 90-degree angle. At both the backswing and finish positions, the tee should point at the ball-target line. Using this drill, hit balls off a tee. In short time, you will be amazed in your swing speed and the consistency of your shots.

Jim McLean on creating lag.

PLAY THE RIGHT-SIZE GRIPS

The bigger the grips, the harder it is for the wrists to hinge. So try to find a circumference that allows an easy wrist hinge.

Justin Leonard Swing Sequence: Hitting a Draw

BUILDING A POWERFUL SWING TO HIT THE BALL HIGHER, FARTHER AND BETTER

My preferred shot has always been a draw. I've never been as long as the bigger hitters, at any level, and I've always need to be better with my longer clubs. Hitting the ball from right-to-left allows me to maximize my power potential especially with the driver.

A good draw swing starts with your weight on the right side, with no slump in your shoulders or back. Set up to the ball with your legs wide and your body in an athletic, "ready" position. Don't slump over the ball or lean your upper body toward the target. Tilt your spine angle so you can really get behind the ball. On the takeaway, keep your club and arms in front of your body as it turns away from the target. At the top, extend your hands away from your head. You don't need to swing past parallel. Power comes from coiling your body and the proper arm extension—not from overswinging.

In the quest for more distance, it's easy to overdo your draw swing. In trying to keep pace with Tiger and the other long hitters on tour, I got into some bad habits. I used to come at the ball from the inside and used too much hand action to square the clubface. My ball flight was too low, and if my timing was off I'd spray it all over. As you can see here, now I'm swinging my arms down away from my body, the clubshaft on-plane and which gives me more clubhead speed and allows me to deliver the clubface to the inside back quadrant of the ball. I stay behind the ball through impact and extend my arms fully on the through-swing. I finish with my belt buckle facing the target and the shaft behind my body and nearly horizontal. A classic finish to a classic draw swing.

Justin Leonard shows you how to hit a draw.

Want to Maximize Distance? First, Learn the Basics of a Draw Swing

PUT SOME KICK IN YOUR SWING

A placekicker almost always "draws" the ball through the goal posts. That's because his foot attacks the ball on an arc from inside the ball-target line. That's the image you should have when you strike a golf ball:

To hit a powerful draw, you must swing the club into the impact zone from the inside. As the above photos show, the foot continues up and back to the inside after impact, which further promotes a powerful hit. That's the image you want during your golf swing.

FINISH LOW TO WORK IT LEFT

When you want to draw the ball, think of finishing with your hands held low and your shoulders on a more horizontal plane. By finishing flatter, you're encouraging your right arm to rotate over the left through impact, which closes the face slightly.

HOW TO FEEL A DRAW

To get your hands and body feeling the proper motion for a right-to-left ball flight, imagine holding a bucket of water with both hands and spilling it over your left shoulder. To do that, you work your right hand over your left as you rotate your body to the left. Your palms are parallel and stay in front of a turning chest, just as they are when you're swinging the club.

A three-time long-drive champion,
Jason Zuback combines raw aggression
with solid technique to launch it over
400 yards. A stable torso supports his huge
windup; through impact his body is behind
the ball and his arms are fully extended.
Just don't try this swing at home!

Shooting in the 70s Means Maximizing Your Clubhead Speed

DON'T BUNT YOUR BALL—SWING FOR THE FENCES

Simply put, clubhead speed equals distance. Without adequate distance, you'll always struggle to break 80, no matter how good your short game. I'm not talking tour speed, but enough to get a man to 240 yards (95 mph with a driver) and a woman to 210 yards (85 mph) off the tee.

    A good way to increase your clubhead speed is to practice letting go and stepping up your swing pace. Make 20 hard driver swings in a row. Do this twice a day. At home, swing a baseball bat as fast as you can 50 times a day. A heavier bat will strengthen your arms and wrists. Make the bat "swish," and step into your swings.

ARE YOU FAST ENOUGH FOR A 2-IRON?

If you can't hit a drive 260 yards, you don't have the swing speed to use a 2-iron. Replace it with a fairway wood. Can't hit it 245? Get rid of that 3-iron, too.

STRAIGHTEN THE ROPE FOR SPEED

This simple rope drill gives instant feedback to help you swing at maximum speed at the optimum moment in the swing—before impact. Hold the end of a three-foot length of rope with your normal grip and get into your stance, as in the small photo below. Make a swing and try to get the rope to straighten just after the point of impact, as I'm doing in the large photo. That means you're generating good speed at the right time.

Jim Goergen on clubhead speed.

Draw: When to Go All Out, and When to Throttle Back

Chuck Cook on
adding distance.

TAKE THIS TIP FROM TENNIS: HIT A TOPSPIN FOREHAND

You may not be able to hit a 300-yard the conventional way, but when the fairways are hard and fast, try the topspin-forehand drive. Essentially you want to make a low-to-high swing and mimic the move you would make to hit a winner in tennis. Tee it low and hit up on the ball, rolling your wrist over (*above*). The ball will come off the club like a rocket, and when it hits the ground, it will keep rolling and rolling and rolling. The lower trajectory gives you more control as well, especially in the wind.

HOW TO AIM WITH A DRAW IN MIND

Learn to aim for a draw. A good rule is to aim 10 yards right of your target. Also, remember a good draw will give you a little more distance, so change your club selection accordingly.

LEAVE YOUR EGO IN THE CAR

Here is Butch Harmon's best advice to good practice and good play: Leave your ego in the car. Whether you're going to practice or play, remember that you're an individual, that you have just 14 clubs, and that you can hit each of those clubs only so far. Learn to live with that. Getting your ego all caught up in how far you hit your driver or other clubs just kills your swing. Use your practice sessions to work on your weaknesses, but when you play realize your limitations and play to your strengths.

By Joe Durant, PGA Tour

MY FIRST TIME

✦ ✦ ✦

The week after the 1998 U.S. Open at Olympic, I played in the Western Open. I knew my game was in pretty good shape, and it was a course—Cog Hill, near Chicago—I like. On the first day, I played pretty solid. But the next day, we had a 90-minute rain delay. Still, when I got on the course, I played very well. I remember finding out on the last hole that day, when there was almost nobody out there, that I was leading the tournament. No TV crews, Nothing. When the TV sportscasters in Pensacola, Fla.—my hometown—found out I was leading the tournament, they were going crazy looking for footage to run. I think one of them actually used popsicle-stick figures to represent me that day.

I started the round four shots back. I played with Lee Janzen, who won the U.S. Open the previous week. We're good friends, so I felt comfortable even though this was my first time near the lead on the final day of a PGA Tour event. I couldn't have played any better. I kept saying to myself, "Just go for it. Don't worry about the consequences of your shots."

I had built a three-shot lead going into 18, and that's the only time in the round I got conservative. I almost hit the ball in the pond trying to play conservatively. Any other year, the wind probably would have blown it into the water, but it was blowing a different way that day. But once I got up near the green, I knew the victory was mine. Even Dave Musgrove, Lee's caddie, gave me a grin after I almost dunked the ball to possibly lose the tournament. It was a memorable win, for sure.

Joe Durant narrowly avoided disaster on the 72nd hole of the 1998 Western Open, his first PGA Tour victory.

Chapter 4

FAIRWAY SHOTS

*How to make solid
and consistent contact
with your fairway woods
and irons. Keep it in
the short grass, and
get it on the green.*

BREAKING 100 90 80

FAIRWAY SHOTS

Advancing the Ball

It's the heart of golf: Hitting the ball off grass, using a full, free-flowing swing. The fairway shot brings all of the essential elements of the game into play. It starts with a consistent preshot routine. Quickly and surely assess the shot at hand: What is your lie? What is your target? What club will best get you safely down the fairway and in position to score well?

While today's tour professional rarely needs to advance the ball down the fairway—all but the longest par 5s seem reachable in two—for the amateur golfer, safe and steady progress toward the hole is a necessary requirement for scoring your best. For the 100-shooter, that means getting the ball airborne every time. Those striving to break 90 often need to tame their ball flight, keeping their shots in the short grass and their ambitions in check. Breaking 80 requires fine-tuning your swing and course-management skills even further, eliminating the loose swings and the mental mistakes that can lead to wasted shots. Your goal is to hit fairway shots that put you in the ideal position to get up and down for par—or birdie.

Previous spread: Tiger Wood hits down and through with a middle iron.

Colin Montgomerie sweeps a fairway wood off the short grass. Easier to hit and get the ball airborne than long irons, today's lofted metal-woods have become a prime scoring weapon for tour pros and amateurs alike.

Making the Transition From Teed-up Shots to Hitting off Grass

GIVE YOURSELF A BREAK: TEE IT UP ON EVERY SHOT

Before you worry about conditions that change with every shot out on the course—like the quality and length of grass your ball is lying on—play all of your fairway shots teed up nicely on a peg.

Play a few rounds this way and you'll notice that you can use the same basic swing for almost all of your full shots from the fairway, and your confidence will grow. Then, hitting from different lies is just a matter of making slight adjustments to that swing to get it to bottom out at the ball.

Once you've mastered hitting from a tee, hit your fairway shots with the ball perched on the front edge of a divot. It will help you build confidence hitting the ball off the ground.

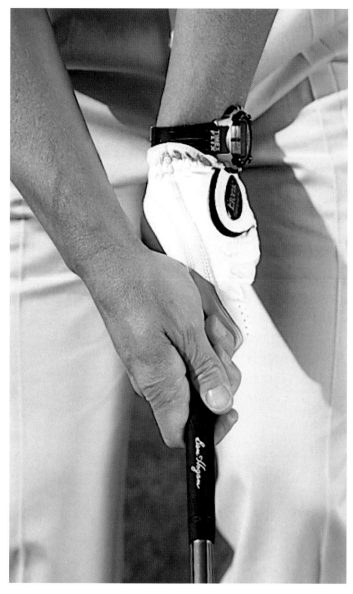

CHECK YOUR GRIP, EVERY TIME

Your grip is something you can never check enough. Consciously reset your grip before each shot you hit at the range and on the course. Otherwise, you'll fall back into bad habits.

THE PERFECT SETUP

You can solve a lot of swing problems before you even start your backswing. Here, my feet and shoulders are parallel to the target line. Since my right hand is on the club lower than my left, my right shoulder is slightly lower than my left. My spine also has a slight tilt to the right, which helps the club approach from a more inside-to-out path on the downswing. Notice that the ball is positioned approximately two inches inside my left heel and my hands are slightly in front of the ball at address.

This setup will allow me to pivot my upper body over my lower body on the backswing, creating coil. The club can now approach on a shallower plane on the downswing, which translates into more consistent contact.

Don Hurter on the address position.

How to Stop Topping Your Shots or Hitting Them Fat

TURN AROUND A STABLE SPINE

Many beginners and high-handicappers overuse their bodies. Instead, they should focus on their hands and arms. Too often, they allow the body to help lift the club up in the backswing, so they fail to maintain the spine tilt they had at address. Result: a flat shoulder turn and inconsistent contact.

To learn the correct feel for maintaining your spine angle, get into a good setup without a club. Then practice a simple arm movement into a solid top-of-swing position in which your spine stays at the same angle it had at address. Don't let your body lift as you swing back. Keep your head very quiet and level—no lifting—as your arms swing back. Now do the same thing with a club.

IDEAL SETUP   NO   YES

Jim McLean on spine angle.

Jane Crafter on angle of attack.

HANDS AHEAD AT IMPACT

When hitting a wood off the fairway, keep your hands slightly ahead of the clubhead into impact, as I'm doing here. It's not a steep descending blow as I would make with an iron, but more of a sweeping motion. Be sure not to flip your hands, as high-handicappers often do to try to help the ball up in the air; you'll just hit the ball fat or top it. Remember: Concentrate on maintaining the posture you had at setup—don't bob up and down.

Eliminate the Big Scores by Playing It Safe from Tee to Green

STRAIGHT SHOOTERS STAY OUT OF TROUBLE

The biggest obstacles to breaking 100 are those occasional high numbers on your scorecard. The next time you play, say, a 400-yard par 4 with lots of trouble all the way down the fairway, suck in your ego and take a 5-iron off the tee. Hit it 150 yards into the fairway, follow it with another 150-yard 5-iron, then a 100-yard wedge into the green. It may not be a Tigeresque strategy, but an easy two-putt for bogey sure beats a tee shot or long approach into the water or the trees. If you simply bogey most of the long par 4s, you'll be well on your way to breaking 100. (Try it on par 5s, too.)

ONE BAD SHOT DOESN'T DESERVE ANOTHER

The key to not making a high score is to never follow a bad shot with a bad decision. If you happen to plunk your tee shot or approach into a water hazard, don't get mad—get even. After you take your one-stroke penalty, don't try to be a hero on your next shot. Concentrate especially hard on getting or keeping the ball safely in play. Rely on your short game—and calm mind—to preserve your score.

HONESTY IS ALWAYS
THE BEST POLICY

Resist the urge to mark a lower score than the one you made. You need a true measure of your skill— and of your improvement. Getting close to a scoring goal is tantalizing. Count all the dubs and penalty strokes, and you'll appreciate the achievement even more.

For a More Consistent Swing, Learn How the Arms Work Together

PRACTICE DRILLS

DIAL UP SOME EXTENSION

I see the bad move in the picture at bottom left more than any other. Instead of taking the club back with the arms as a unit, I'm letting my right arm collapse toward my body. This makes for a short, narrow backswing and a poor turn. Take a large rubber band (like the kind that grocery stores use to bunch asparagus together) and place it over the middle of your forearms, as I did in the picture on the right. Hit some soft shots with the rubber band in place. If you want to keep the skin on your arms, you'll have to make a smooth, one-piece take-away, like in the "Yes" photo below. You'll hit it longer and straighter.

Randy Smith on staying connected.

NO YES

YES

NO

USE YOUR RUBBER BAND TO CHOP THE 'CHICKEN WING'

Even good players sometimes make the mistake you see here on the left when they try to hit it hard. My arms have separated from each other through impact, and I've dramatically dipped my right shoulder toward the ball. I'm going to hit it fat or thin from here. Hitting full shots with the rubber band in place keeps the arms where they should be through impact—helping you make that nice, solid downward strike, the way I am in the photo above.

A ROCK-SOLID TAKEAWAY

Your abdominal muscles are the core of your swing. Focus on your abs and use them to start your backswing. Your hands and arms will follow in unison.

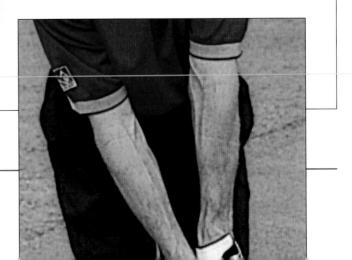

Develop a Preshot Routine and Follow It on Every Shot

Gale Peterson on preshot routine.

GOOD SWINGS START WITH A PERFECT ROUTINE

Learn to rely on a simple, short preshot routine. Make it purposeful, too. Set your aim from behind the ball and focus on an intermediate target (*below*). Then make a practice swing that is a true dress rehearsal for your real swing. Brush the grass on your practice swing and even swing at a leaf or spot on the ground to simulate impact. That's better than a half-hearted practice swing six inches off the ground, aimed at nothing.

DR. BOB SAYS: STAY WITH YOUR ROUTINE AND FOCUS ON YOUR TARGET

Some people think I make too big a deal over preshot routine. They also think it slows the game down. Neither is true. A preshot routine should not be slow, and I don't think you can make too big a deal of it. Developing an effortlessly consistent preshot routine has two major benefits: First, the routine turns off your conscious mind, which, if active, disrupts your ability to hit a solid shot. Second, it gets you focused on the target and nothing else.

PICK UP THE PACE

You can shoot 120 and still play with low-handicappers as long as you are fast, safe and courteous. There are a lot of elements to a good preshot routine, but they should be done quickly. If it takes longer than 15 seconds, then you've taken too much time. Be aware of how long you're taking, and pick up your ball when you've hit too many.

Sharpen Course-Management Skills to Score Your Best on Long Holes

GO FOR IT, BUT DON'T FORCE IT

When I'm playing in pro-ams, I notice my amateur partners often don't take enough club to reach their target, whether it's to clear a creek in the fairway or get to the green. To make matters worse, they try to hit the ball too hard. What you want to do is make a relaxed swing. You'll end up hitting the ball farther than by forcing it. If you're going uphill or into the wind, take an extra club or two. Once you've chosen your club, be committed and swing confidently.

FROM THE FAIRWAY, NO 3-WOODS

Most 15-plus handicappers can't advance a 3-wood off the ground or regularly keep it in the fairway. A 5-wood is more forgiving. Choose it instead.

LAY BACK, DON'T LAY UP

The worst mistake you can make when playing it safe is to get greedy and lay the ball up too close to (or put it in) a water hazard. Think "lay back," not "lay up" to stay away from trouble.

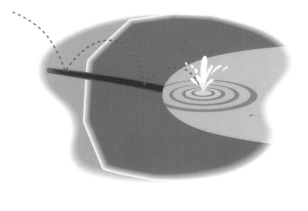

Beth Bauer on taking enough club.

FORGET PRIDE—USE A 7-WOOD

There are a bunch of tour pros using 7-woods and a bunch of amateurs carrying 2- and 3-irons. What's wrong with this picture? For most amateurs, says Scott Davenport, the only benefit of a 3-iron is that it's good for punching out from the trees. A 7-wood gets the ball airborne easier and carries it farther.

Swing Check: Ingrain the Proper Feel of the First Move Down

THE MAGIC OF THE DOMINANT-ARM DRILL

The No. 1 drill that Jim McLean uses at his golf schools is the right-arm-only drill (left-arm for left-handers). Your dominant side is the hand and arm you eat and throw with. It's the key to a powerful, consistent golf swing.

Practice swinging a club with your dominant arm. Let your elbow come away from your body on the backswing for a wide arc (*inset*), then narrow the arc coming down (*large photo*). A tee placed in the butt of the handle should point downward halfway into the backswing and toward the target halfway down.

WIDE BACK

NARROW DOWN

BEAT AN EARLY RELEASE BY KEEPING THE UMBRELLA CLOSED

Imagine swinging a folded umbrella from the top of your backswing. If the initial movement is sideways first, the umbrella would open early (*below*). If the initial movement is downward, the umbrella would stay closed until later (*left*). If your hands are to the side of your head when you're fully turned at the top, they can travel straight down at the start of the downswing, which creates more speed. If the hands are behind the head, they have to move out before they can go down—a casting move that's a power killer. Remember: Hands downward instead of clubhead around.

YES

NO

Tom Ness on the first move down.

When to Use a Long Iron—and How to Get the Most Out of It

TWO TIPS TO HELP YOU HIT YOUR LONG IRONS WELL

It's great that lofted fairway woods have become popular. But someday you'll be playing in the wind and want the lower trajectory of a long iron. Here are two tips to hitting a long iron well:

Complete your backswing. The most common long-iron fault I see is that players don't complete their backswing turn. Be a little more deliberate as you turn back, to really wind your shoulders up. Try to get your front shoulder turned behind the ball. With a club held across your chest, practice turning back until the club actually points behind the ball.

Swing within yourself. Many people believe they have to hit the ball harder with a long iron. You don't. All you have to do is hit it solid, and the ball will jump off the clubface. So swing a little smoother— even a little easier—to make sure you finish your backswing, and then make good contact.

YES

Butch Harmon on the long-iron swing.

NO

SWEEP AWAY YOUR LONG-IRON DOUBTS

Even the best players fear long irons. Why do you think so many tour players are hitting high-lofted fairway woods and driving irons? But although long irons are probably the most difficult clubs to use, remember that if you can groove a 2-iron, you can hit any club in the bag. The best tip for long irons is to try to sweep the ball off the turf. Make as thin a divot as possible. A steep downswing makes an already low-lofted long iron even lower.

USE IRONS IN THE WIND

If you know before the round that it's going to be a windy day, take that 7-wood out of the bag and replace it with a 3- or 4-iron. It's much easier to keep the ball down with a long iron than it is with a wood.

Janet Coles on grooving a 2-iron.

Fine-Tune Your Thinking, Your Swing—and Your Tools of the Trade

Rick Smith on shot strategy.

DON'T ALWAYS TAKE THE LONG WAY HOME

The 270-yard marker below doesn't automatically mean you pull a 3-wood and try to bust one up by the green. Many times, that kind of shot will only bring trouble into play. Even if you hit it well, you'll leave yourself with a half-wedge approach. Try the smarter shot, which, in this case, takes the water on the left out of play and still gives you a good chance to make par or birdie. Take a 6-iron and lay up. You'll have a comfortable, full wedge or 9-iron into the green.

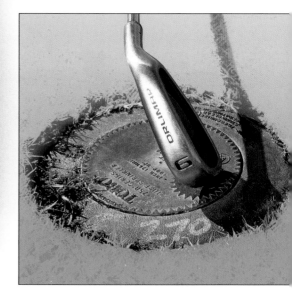

CUT DOWN ON FAIRWAY MIS-HITS

Better players hit down on the ball with fairway woods from a tight lie. They play the ball back in their stance a bit and "squeeze" it off the turf. You'll cut down on topped shots.

KNOW YOUR EQUIPMENT

CHECK THE SPECS ON YOUR CLUBS

The importance of a custom fit to the better player is undeniable. Jack Nicklaus always had the loft of his irons dialed in to deliver the ball a specific distance. In most iron sets today, the lofts are pretty good, so focus on the lie angle of your irons and make sure they're not set too flat. If they are, the toe is going to catch the ground first and send the clubface wide open. Better to err on the side of too upright. The proper shaft weight also is important; too light or too heavy affects the feel of the club. Flex is not that critical in your irons; either an R or an S will suffice.

By Adam Scott, PGA Tour

MY FIRST TIME

◆ ◆ ◆

I remember feeling pretty nervous on the final day of the 2001 Dunhill Championship because it was my first time leading a professional event going into the last round. Being paired with Justin Rose was really good for me, though. I felt I could match up with him better because we're about the same age—as opposed to being paired with an older player like Nick Faldo.

At one point I was four strokes up in the round, but after a couple three-putts I fell one back. That was before I birdied three of the last five holes to win by a stroke. On the 14th hole I made a real snakey putt that had to be close to 30 feet. Making that one really got me going.

I didn't really think about it at the time, but that was how you want to win a golf tournament. Making those shots, and coming back from being down after leading early in the final round was pretty clutch. I really felt like I earned my first victory and that it wasn't handed to me.

Adam Scott, the svelte young Australian, is one of the Tour's long hitters, averaging nearly 300 yards off the tee.

Chapter 5

PITCH SHOTS

Scoring well requires
pitch shots that stop
close to the hole. Master the
mini-swing to turn
short shots around the green
into big winners.

PITCH SHOTS

Mastering the Mini-Swing

Learning how to be more consistent with your short shots not only saves strokes around the green, it also rewards with better rhythm and contact on your full swings. The fundamentals are the same: A balanced, "ready" position at address, synchronized movement with your arms and body, and a firm yet flowing motion through impact. Crisp contact is assured with a downward blow to the back of the ball, nipping it off the turf.

Sound technique isn't enough, though. Successful pitch shots also require a practiced blend of imagination and strategy. You have to learn to think your way around the green. Making better decisions in your short game is going to do only one thing—help you shoot lower scores.

Picking the right short-game shot for the situation is the difference between the 80s-shooter and a player who can get into the mid-70s. Even tour players can't always save par when they leave themselves five- and six-footers after mediocre pitches. The beauty of the mini-swing is that any golfer can master it, as long as you follow the proper advice.

Previous spread: Greg Norman hits a high, soft pitch from a tricky sidehill lie.

LPGA superstar Annika Sorenstam has one of the game's most fluid and efficient swings. Her driver swing is simply a longer version of her pitch-shot technique. The result: year in, year out she leads her peers in scoring average.

Learn the Basics of the Mini-Swing by Blending Technique and Feel

KEEP YOUR WEIGHT LEFT

The key to pitches and short wedge shots is a 60/40 weight distribution. At setup, 60 percent of your weight should be on your left side. When you dangle the club from your chin, the shaft will align well ahead of the ball. Notice how this plays out at address (*inset*), with the hands leading the clubhead. From here, you can hit the ball with a crisp descending blow, using the loft of the club to get the ball airborne.

Jane Crafter on balance.

SOMEWHERE OVER THE. . .

Think of the arc of a rainbow as you prepare for a pitch shot. Its trajectory is similar, and using imagery helps mentally. You can watch as the ball plops into the pot of gold.

LET THE WEDGE'S LOFT PROVIDE HEIGHT

A pitch shot is vital when you need to get the ball up to an elevated green or over a bunker or other hazard. Avoid "helping" the ball up; don't make a scooping motion. Keep the image in your mind of the left arm and shaft forming a straight line just after impact, not before. Square the clubface to the target line and trust the loft of the club to do the work of getting the ball in the air.

Jack Lumpkin on trajectory.

Improve Your Distance Control by Improving Your Short-Game Touch

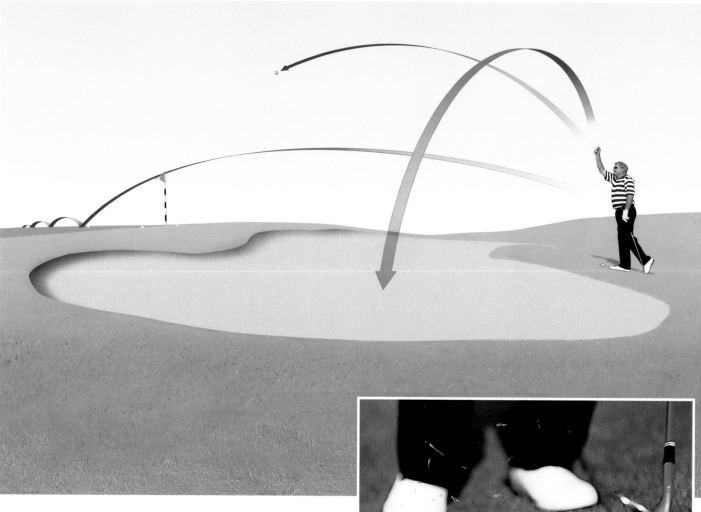

GIVE SHORT SHOTS SOME FEELING

Your short game will be an asset only after you begin to develop a feel for distance. One way to do this is to practice tossing balls to a flag on a practice green. The more you do it, the more you'll match a certain body feeling to a certain length shot. Then, when you get on the course, imagine what type of toss would best fit the shot you have, then select the club and the swing that will allow you to duplicate that trajectory.

ANOTHER WAY TO FEEL IT

Good players rehearse the right feeling for a shot. You can do this, too, by getting in the habit of brushing the same amount of grass with each practice swing.

LEARN WHICH SWING EQUALS WHICH DISTANCE

Partial shots can hurt your score the most if you are uncertain how to match a backswing and follow-through to a certain distance. You really only need to develop a half swing, where the hands are below waist level, and a three-quarter swing, where the hands are just above waist level. Anything less is a chip; anything more is a full swing. Strive to make the shortened swings natural, not cut off. Keep your lower body stable, and make sure you swing through to a full finish.

Gale Peterson on distance control.

Practice Time Spent on Pitch Shots Will Benefit Your Full Swing

PRACTICE DRILLS

LET THE BUNKER BE YOUR FRIEND

Most ranges these days have bunkers in front of some of their target greens. Next time you practice, work on hitting balls into a bunker that's 30 to 80 yards away. These bunkers serve as perfect targets for learning distance control, and the next time you have to hit over a bunker on the course, you'll have more confidence about what club you need to use and how hard to swing.

HOME SCHOOLING

Take 20 minutes to practice your short game by pitching into an inverted umbrella in your backyard. Once back on the course, you'll be pleased with your newfound accuracy.

John Elliott Jr. on accuracy.

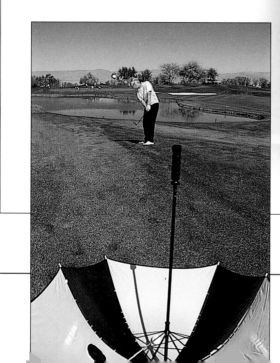

Rick Smith on timing.

GET YOUR SWING IN SYNC FOR CRISP CONTACT

To keep all of your parts—the arms, shoulders, hips and legs—working in the right order, try this drill: With your left hand anchored to the middle of your chest, make a full turn away from the ball. Your arm and chest should move away together, as shown above. Then make a smooth downswing and hit the ball. Swing your arm faster than your body, and you'll skull it. Drive your body too much, and the club will hit the ground behind the ball, chunking it.

Learn to Hit Your Pitch Shots High so They Land Softly on the Green

KEEP THE FACE OPEN THROUGH IMPACT

The pitch shot is really the beginning of your full swing. The main difference is that you have the clubface slightly open throughout the motion. You can't hit a high pitch with a closed face. A pitch shot is a sweeping motion, sliding the club under the ball. Don't take much of a divot, and don't choke down on the club for a high pitch.

Hank Haney on pitching it high.

KNOW YOUR EQUIPMENT

CLOSE THE GAP

To give your short game the most flexibility, you should have three wedges in your bag, with a 4- to 5-degree difference in loft angle between them. Have a pro check the lofts to get them right. Generally speaking, each degree of loft on your wedges translates to two to four yards in carry distance. Shoot for a 10-yard gap between each wedge.

FIVE KEYS TO PITCHING IT HIGHER

Lobbing a high pitch shot can be useful, but be forewarned: The higher the trajectory, the greater the risk. Here are five keys to hitting your pitch shots higher:

• Open the face of your sand wedge so that the face points slightly right of your target.

• Aim a little left of your target.

• Open your stance.

• Because you're contacting the ball with a glancing blow, you'll need a longer-than-normal swing, similar to the length of swing you'd make if you were in a bunker from the same distance.

• Never swing "at the ball," but to the end of your follow-through.

Add Another Element to Your Game: The High, Soft Lob Shot

Josh Zander on the lob shot.

TAKE THE WRISTS OUT OF THE LOB SHOT

Most people use too much wrist cock (*right*) to hit the lob shot. You don't need much. Too much wrist action makes it hard to control your distance and gives you more chances to lay sod over the ball. Instead, make the swing an arm and body motion. Maintain the loft on the club and take a bigger swing, with just a little wrist cock. It's easier to control the big muscles, and they'll help you hit these delicate shots more consistently.

WHY ONE CLUB IS BETTER THAN MANY

Phil Mickelson has built his short game around one club. You'll hit more good shots by totally knowing one club than you will by trying unfamiliar shots with different clubs. Judy Rankin has used this Wilson R90 sand wedge for the last 30 years. It may look like a relic, but it's tried and true. Be loyal to clubs that work.

If a scoring club works for you, then stick with it.

HOW TO BUY A HIGHER SHOT

Equipment can help you hit the high lob, says Hank Haney. Most companies now manufacture wedges that have up to 62 degrees of loft. Put one in your bag and take out the 1- or 2-iron you rarely hit. Practice your distance control with the ultra-high-lofted wedge by varying the length of the swing and the amount you open the clubface. With so much loft, you may find you don't need to open the face much to get the trajectory you need to fly the ball over trouble. But keep one thing constant: Play the ball forward in your stance.

TO LOB IT, JUST GET LAZY

To hit a high, soft-landing shot, relax. Make a longer swing, but make it lazier, too. Think of Fred Couples' smooth tempo and light touch. Swing slower and slide the club under the ball, letting the club's momentum do the work.

Left-handed superstar Phil Mickelson possesses
one of the most creative, and accurate,
short games ever. His trademark shot is the flop,
the sky-high lob that lands softly.

You've Mastered the Basic High Lob. Now Try These Specialty Shots

THE TOUR-FLOP SAND WEDGE FROM ROUGH

This shot is played from deep, gnarly rough around the green, especially when there is little green to work with. It's a high, soft lob that pancakes when it hits the green and just stops dead.

Secret No. 1: Aim a full five or six inches behind the ball. Play the ball forward in your stance. Use an open 56-degree sand wedge or a 60-degree lob wedge. Secret No. 2: Pivot on your back leg. Now swing to a full finish. The result will astound your playing partners.

Jim McLean on hitting from deep rough.

HOW TO HIT A PITCH THAT BITES

If you can produce backspin on your pitches, be more aggressive with them. To hit pitches with more spin, strengthen your left-hand grip and hold the left hand firm through impact. You'll be able to hit pitch shots that bounce once and check.

LOBBING IT FROM A TIGHT LIE

If you have some confidence with your lob wedge, you can hit a lob from a tight lie. Play the ball back in your stance, off your right toe, and set your weight and hands slightly forward. Since playing the ball back reduces the effective loft of your wedge, open the clubface to get that loft back. Opening the face also creates more bounce, so the leading edge doesn't dig. Then try to clip the ball cleanly (don't take a divot), and keep the finish low.

Don Hurter on hitting from short grass.

Practice the Shots You Need on the Course, from Realistic Conditions

MIX IT UP ON THE RANGE, LIKE THE REAL THING

Anybody who practices from one spot long enough can get really good at one kind of shot—say, a 30-yard pitch to a certain flag on the practice green, from a nice, cushy lie. The real thing isn't quite like that. You never know what you're going to get out on the course. Make your practice more like actual on-course conditions. Drop a few balls and hit them, then move to a different spot and hit to the same target. Change the lie and the shot to keep your mind engaged.

Randy Smith on practicing smart.

USE A SOFTER BALL
Average players should use a distance ball. Low-handicap players, for whom control is more important, need softer, high-spin balls.

By Stuart Appleby, PGA Tour

MY FIRST TIME

◆ ◆ ◆

My first win on the PGA Tour was an adventure. I missed the cut at Doral in 1997, so I did a lot of practicing on the range leading into the Honda Classic the next week. I didn't know what was going to happen, but I got something out of that range time and really liked my swing. I went into the Honda not with huge expectations, but certainly with confidence. The greens were fantastic, and I like how windy it was. It felt like Australia and those conditions back home.

I was in contention all week. Then on Sunday, we played 36 holes, and I played really good golf and made a lot of putts. Then I had a pitch-in for eagle on No. 14, a par 5, that tied me for the lead. Then came the fun part: I had to sit in the clubhouse and nervously watch as Michael Bradley holed about a 40-foot putt on No. 17 for par to stay within one shot of me. He then hit a big drive on No. 18, and his approach landed 20 feet from the hole. It was pretty nerve-racking watching that putt, because you can't do anything about it. But it missed, and I won. I remember stopping for a moment and thinking, "Here I am: Last week, I missed the cut, and now I'm watching one guy miss a putt for me to win a tournament." It was pretty wild.

But the one thing I remember most was the drive back home to Orlando with [his late wife] Renay. That was pretty awesome. It was a huge turning point in my career. It was like I had finally arrived on tour.

Raised on a dairy farm in Australia, Stuart Appleby learned to play golf hitting from paddock to paddock after his chores were finished.

Chapter 6

CHIP SHOTS

Get up and down from
just off the green by getting
your chip shots close to
the hole. It's the shot in golf
all golfers can, and should,
learn to master.

BREAKING
100 90 80
CHIP SHOTS

Getting It Close to the Hole

Not even the best players in the world hit every green in regulation, yet they still manage to break 70 routinely. The chip shot is the ultimate stroke-saver, the shot in your bag that can turn a possible bogey back into a par in one crisply struck hit.

The stroke itself is a simple one—the shortest of swings taken from a narrow stance. The key to successful chipping is keeping your hands ahead of the clubhead and hitting the ball with a crisp, downward blow. Your goal is to keep the ball low and get it rolling on the green like a putt as soon as possible. Improving your chipping skills is a matter of knowing which club to use depending on the amount of green you have to work with, and learning to play the right amount of break and speed.

This is a shot from a good lie, with no obstacles between you and the hole. And with practice to refine your swing motion and touch, there's no reason why you can't become an expert chipper who expects to make your fair share of shots from just off the green.

Previous spread: Tom Watson takes dead aim from just off the green.

*Golf fans think "power"
when they talk of Tiger.
But it's his short-game
skills and creativity that
separate him from the rest.*

When to Chip, Which Club to Use, and How to Hit It

USE THE CHIP SHOT AS CONDITIONS DICTATE

With a chip shot, the ball flies a short way—like over some rough—and then rolls a longer distance than it flew. Here are the essentials: Narrow your stance (less than shoulder width), position the ball inside your left heel (*right*) with your weight slightly on your left side. There may be a slight pivoting of the knees, hips and shoulders on the backswing, but there should be minimal maneuvering of the club with your hands. The left wrist stays flat on the follow-through.

Jack Lumpkin on chipping technique.

DROP THAT LOB WEDGE!

Most high-handicappers should scrap the lob wedge. Instead of lofting shots, hit down on your wedges and finish low and short. The ball will fly lower with more spin and more control. Retrieve the 60-degree wedge when you're breaking 80.

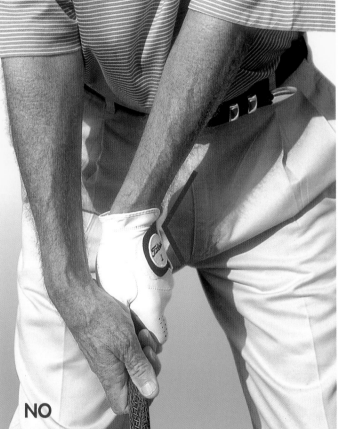

NO

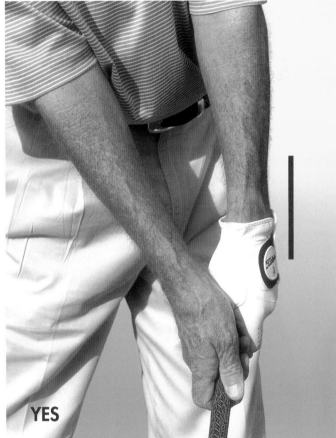

YES

YOUR LEFT WRIST IS THE KEY TO HITTING CRISP, LOW CHIPS

Most mis-hits occur because the left wrist breaks down just before impact. Beginners think they have to lift the ball in the air by scooping it, often by flipping the left wrist at impact (*left*). To hit the ball crisply, try maintaining the impact position shown here (*right*). Your left wrist should remain flat and should be slightly closer to the target than the clubhead is. The ball will fly low and stay on line.

Refine the Basic Chipping Stroke by Following Simple Fundamentals

David Leadbetter
on ball position.

'BUTTON UP' YOUR CHIPS

Make sure the buttons on your shirt are in front of the ball. If you are leaning to the left, you'll be in good position to hit down on the ball.

PINCH THE BALL

It's important to keep your hands and club moving in the same direction toward the hole. At impact, have the low point of the chipping stroke occur on the target side of the ball. Finish with the clubhead below the hands.

Todd Anderson
on impact position.

Don Hurter on club selection.

HOW TO SELECT THE RIGHT CHIPPING CLUB

On most chip shots, your goal is to get the ball rolling on the green as soon as possible. Pick the club that will land the ball about 10 feet onto the green and make it roll to the hole. As a rule, an 8-iron will fly one-third its total distance to the hole and roll two-thirds. A pitching wedge has a half-and-half air-to-ground ratio, while a sand wedge will fly two-thirds and roll one-third.

Make Your Share of Shots From Just Off the Green by Adding New Tricks

LET THE LIE DETERMINE YOUR STANCE ON GREENSIDE SHOTS

The basic rule for chipping is, the worse your lie, the farther back in your stance you need to play the ball and the more loft you have to use. Both of the shots shown here are the same distance to the flag. But for the shot on the left, the ball and club are tangled in deep grass. Use your sand wedge, and play the ball well behind your back foot, so you can bring the club down on the ball without having to drag it through a lot of grass. The sole of the sand wedge helps the club slide through the grass and the loft gets the ball airborne.

The lie is perfect for the shot on the right. Chip with a 7-iron, playing the ball nearer your front heel. The ball should hop over the fringe and roll like a putt when it lands on the green.

PLAY BREAK ON CHIPS

At this level, you're good enough to make your share of chip shots. Maximize your chances by reading what the ball will do after you land it on the green. On a running shot, you'll have to account for more break. High shots take less. Treat these shots as you would a putt by gauging green speed and contour.

Mark Winkley on holing more chip shots.

TAKE DEAD AIM

For a good player, a chip from a good lie just off the green should always have a chance to go in. To practice your setup and aim, lay a club down in the fringe on a line between you and the hole. (Remember to take the break into account.) Practice flying your chips just over the club, right on line. Work to finish each chip with your clubhead directly over the target line.

SINK IT WITH A FAIRWAY WOOD

A lofted wood isn't only a good option for a tee shot to a narrow fairway. You can take advantage of its wide, flat sole for shots from unusual lies around the green, too. It works great from tightly mowed areas with steep inclines or from patchy grass in the first cut. Set up with your shoulders slightly forward. Slide the club through the shot, just as you would for a putting stroke. Don't release or hit at the ball. Just keep your hands quiet as much as possible.

To Take Your Game to the Next Level, Think—and Act—Like a Pro

PRACTICE DOING IT WRONG

Most of us make the same mistake over and over—for example, hitting all our chips long and left. A good way to break that kind of pattern is to practice missing in different places. In the drill shown here, I'm trying to hit chips short, long left and right—but not to the pin itself. This drill not only helps your touch, it will help you experiment to find a swing that will get the ball close to the hole when you want to.

FEELING GROOVY

You need to have clean grooves to make good, clean contact. That's how you can control your irons and hit those little spin shots with bite on them. Use the tip of a tee as your tool so at least the critical bottom four or five grooves on your scoring clubs are cleaned out.

John Elliott Jr. on developing feel.

THE MENTAL SIDE

BE AS FOCUSED AS A PRO

To play your best, you need to be conscientious. My friend on the left here would play better if he took more care with his clothes, his clubs and maybe even his fitness. That's me on the right. I try to dress neatly and have everything in place before I play. To force yourself to concentrate more seriously on your preparations and your game, try to play some real tournament golf— not just fun games with your buddies.

It's important to associate with players who are likely to help you. You want to play with people who think and react positively to situations. Every time you play, you want to learn something by being around them.

Avoid complainers and grumblers whenever possible. And be aware that you might fall into this category, which steals from the enjoyment of others.

You can learn the most from better players, who have more consistency, experience and confidence. They have mastered what you are trying to learn, and they can teach it to you indirectly.

By Jeff Sluman, PGA Tour

MY FIRST TIME

◆ ◆ ◆

I remember distinctly shooting 79 for the first time. I was 10 years old, and I was playing with my dad and my brother at Oak Orchard Country Club in Rochester, N.Y. I obviously couldn't hit it very far, but I was a pretty good player. It was a short, tricky course, but I managed a 38 on the front. Then I hit one out-of-bounds on the back and made a double bogey. Coming to 18, I knew I had to make a par to break 80. Of course, when you're 10, there's no such thing as nerves. You know you've always got another day coming. (And there have been plenty of times when I was 17, 27 and 37 that I wished I had the short-game nerves I had when I was 10.) But I made my par to shoot 79. My dad called it in the next day, but they spelled my name wrong in the newspaper.

Since joining the PGA Tour in 1983, Jeff Sluman has won six tournaments, including the 1988 PGA Championship, and more than $14 million in earnings.

Chapter 7

PUTTING

It's the simple truth:
The quickest—and easiest—
way to lower scores is to take
fewer shots on the
putting green. Here's how.

PUTTING

Developing Technique and Feel

How important is putting to your overall score? You do the math: A golfer who hits every green in regulation and two-putts every hole will shoot a 72—and in the process take exactly one-half his or her total shots for the day on the putting green. Players striving to break 100 or 90 typically take 40 putts or more during 18 holes; keep in mind that even tour players who shoot in the 60s are likely to take around 30 putts per round.

With at least 4 out of every 10 strokes in a given round taking place on the putting green, it's no wonder the best teachers place such emphasis on mastering "the game within a game." Improve your performance with the putter, and your total score will drop dramatically.

What's more, good touch in your putting game makes up for shortcomings in other areas. After all, every stroke counts the same, whether it's a 300-yard drive or a three-foot putt. While most golfers will never be able to blast a tee shot 300 yards, virtually all players can, with practice, make most of the three-footers they face—and sink their fair share of longer putts as well. The secret is in mastering a repetitive stroke and developing the right amount of "feel."

Previous spread: Fred Couples attempts to roll in a long, big-breaking putt.

Throughout his career, Tiger Woods has demonstrated an uncanny ability to make crucial putts at critical moments. Luck? Hardly: His success is the result of a consistent pre-putt routine and stroke, coupled with great imagination and focus.

First, Build a Repeatable Putting Stroke and Consistent Pre-Putt Routine

KEEP YOUR WRISTS FIRM FOR A SOLID PUTTING STROKE

The most common mistake for club golfers is to overuse the wrists on longer putts (*below*). To eliminate too much hitting action in your wrists, use your shoulders and arms to create motion. Retain the triangle formed by the arms and wrists, as in the "Yes" photo, through to the finish. The butt of the club should point to the left hip, not toward your belt buckle. Using your arms and shoulders will give you consistent roll and more reliable distance control.

NO

YES

Don Hurter on firm wrists.

THE MENTAL SIDE

FOLLOW BURKE'S BASICS OF PUTTING

Jackie Burke, one of Jim McLean's teaching mentors, always stressed these three basics of putting: tempo, calmness and imagination. As you approach a putt, walk rhythmically—not too fast, not too slow. Take a deep breath, and go through your routine with a kind of relaxed focus on the task at hand. Finally, picture the line and imagine making a great stroke.

ESTABLISH A PUTTING ROUTINE

All good putters have a regular putting routine. The discipline to follow the same pattern before each putt gives you the consistency you need for solid putting. After you've decided your line, align the putter with your right arm and sight the putterface to your target. Next, put both hands on the grip, look at the target, look at the ball, and roll it. To develop better feel, try practice putting while looking at the target rather than at the ball.

Todd Anderson on consistency.

TO READ BREAK, GO WITH THE FLOW

Reading greens is an acquired skill, but here's a quick tip for long putts: Imagine how water would flow off the green. That's how the putt will break.

Refine Your Distance Control and Improve Your Alignment

FRAME YOUR PUTTING STROKE

Too many beginners try to push or pull a putt to get it on target instead of starting square and trusting the stroke. They sideswipe the ball, send it off line and have a heck of a time with distance control. Simplify your putting by getting square. Picture a framing square as it relates to your putter and your line. The vertical part of the tool should be parallel to the face of your putter, and the horizontal part should be parallel to the target line. Keep the putter on line and the face square, and the ball will go where you aim it.

LET'S HEAR IT FOR...YOU!

Accurate long putting is more difficult than golfers think. The next time you two-putt from 50 feet, give yourself a quiet round of applause. The positive reinforcement helps.

Beth Bauer on distance control.

LAG WITHOUT A CLUB

One of the best ways to practice your lag putting is to drop your putter and roll the ball on the green by hand. Tossing a ball toward the hole allows you to focus on judging the distance instead of worrying about your stroke. It's a more instinctive move than a mechanical one. You're also rocking your shoulders in the same way you would during a good stroke. Notice, too, that your best tosses come without any extra hand action. That's a great thing to remember when you pick up the putter again—make your stroke a slow, precise and simple one, with no extra hand action.

Randy Smith on improving your touch.

LEARN TO ROLL THE BALL THE RIGHT DISTANCE

On putts of 12 feet or more, don't get hung up on direction. Concentrate instead on distance. The key is letting yourself roll the ball to the hole. Don't worry about aim or how you're gripping the putter, just focus on distance. Ideally the ball should have enough pace to finish 18 inches past the hole, but learn to die the ball at the hole first. Remember, we're talking about breaking 100, we're not talking about holing more long putts. We're talking about eliminating three-putts by lagging it close.

Practice These Simple Drills to Cut Down on Three-Putt Greens

PRACTICE DRILLS

LONG PUTTS: 'CLIMB THE LADDER' TO BETTER FEEL

Good touch comes from learning what length stroke produces what length putt. On a sloping area of the green place tees about 40 to 50 feet apart, with five golf clubs spaced about three feet apart from each other, midway between the tees. Starting with uphill putts, get your first putt to stop between the first and second clubs, your second putt between the second and third clubs and so on, "up the ladder." Repeat the drill for the downhill putts. Continue until you get all the way up and down the ladder without hitting a putt too long or too short. Make a practice stroke while looking at the target, and then try to repeat that length stroke on the putt itself. When it gets too easy, try the drill while putting with your eyes closed.

SHORT PUTTS: PRACTICE A PERFECT DOZEN TO INSTILL CONFIDENCE

Solid short putting is a function of confidence, and confidence comes from making a lot of putts, as in the drill at right. Starting a putter-length from the hole, place 12 tees around the cup in four sets of three, each a grip length from the preceding tee. Ideally, one set will be uphill, one downhill, one a right-to-left breaker and the other a left-to-right. Make 12 putts in a row and you can go home. Miss one and start back at the beginning.

Chuck Cook on target practice.

'CAN' YOUR PUTTS

A good drill: Putt at a soda can sticking out of the hole. This target looks big because it's above ground, but it's actually smaller than the hole.

FIND A REPEATING RHYTHM TO END THREE-PUTTS

If you're not breaking 100, you're probably three-putting more holes than not. Your stroke is probably all over the place. Stroke your putts with an even beat for a repeating motion. Think to yourself "back and through" as you do so. The length of your stroke will change, but focus on keeping your rhythm constant. For a drill, putt three balls from 10 feet away and try to keep them within a three-foot circle of the hole. Move out by five-foot increments, and continue the drill.

Todd Anderson on putting rhythm.

Develop Your Ability to Judge the Slope and Speed of the Putting Surface

Don Hurter on reading greens.

FOLLOW YOUR FEET
FOR SPEED AND FEEL

Read greens two ways—with your eyes and with your feet. By stepping off the distance of your putts, as I am doing here, you will know the exact distance to the hole and sense any changes in the slope as you walk along the line. Then, getting as low as you can, check out the putt from behind the ball to get a sense of break, as I am doing in the small photo. You can do this while others in your group are putting.

Tom Ness on the proper stance.

IMPROVE YOUR PUTTING SETUP AND ALIGNMENT

Before you make a stroke, the biggest challenge in putting is translating what you see—the line of the putt and the hole itself—into what you do. Most players step into their stance first, then align the clubface, which usually means the clubface is pointed too far right of the target. The stroke then has to compensate. To set up more accurately, start by aiming your putter first, with your right foot placed even with the ball (*left photo*), which gives you a 90-degree angle to the target line to use as a reference. Then align your feet, placing your left foot next to the right and adjusting the right foot away from the target (*right photo*). Now I'm in a balanced set-up position, with the ball toward the front of your stance.

GRIP THE PUTTER LIGHTLY

If you can't seem to get any feel for your putts, try gripping the putter lightly in your fingers, not your palms.

'TRIANGULATE' YOUR PUTTS

Always read putts from three angles: from behind the ball, from behind the hole and from halfway between the ball and the hole on the low side of the line.

Banish Three-Putts for Good by Controlling Your Putting Tempo

PUTT WITH A PENDULUM-LIKE STROKE

All good putters have a sameness of pace to their stroke. This allows them to find the proper length for their stroke for any given putt. The length of swing and the weight of the putterhead create a natural pendulum-like acceleration through the ball. Good putters approach putting as though the ball is merely in the way of a smoothly flowing stroke.

THINK OF EVERY CUP AS THE GRAND CANYON

In putting, a bad attitude—"I'll never make it"—is worse than bad mechanics. Don't fear success. Try to make every putt (within reason) and worry about the next putt later. You'll have fewer misses.

Judy Rankin on tempo.

TEST BALLS FOR FEEL

If the putting greens where you play the most are firm and fast, use a soft-cover ball. Most soft-cover balls spin more on iron shots, which will help keep your approach shots closer to the hole. Many good putters prefer the feel of a soft-cover ball (which is the result primarily of sound). Test a variety of balls to see which ball model works best for you.

ROCK YOUR SHOULDERS STRAIGHT UP AND DOWN

People who aren't breaking 90 often are so eager to follow the progress of their putts, they open their shoulders through impact ("*No*" photo). The result? Inconsistent contact and direction. Instead, stroke putts by rocking your shoulders up and down, keeping them parallel to the target line. To ingrain the proper feeling, hold the front of your right shoulder with your left hand ("*Yes*" photo). Stroke putts with just the right arm; focus on moving your shoulders straight up and down, as if they were a connected, pendulum-like unit.

David Leadbetter on the pendulum stroke.

Make Practice Sessions on the Putting Green More Fun—and Productive

PRACTICE DRILLS

MAKE SIX ACES FOR CONFIDENCE

The "Six Aces" drill is really simple, says Jim McLean. Just take 12 balls, drop them 15 to 20 feet from the cup and keeping putting them, 12 at a time, until you make six out of 12. This drill increases the putting confidence of players at all levels. High-handicappers learn to make more mid-length par putts, and low-handicappers see they can make more of those birdie putts than they thought.

Bob Rotella on putting confidence.

GET IN THE HABIT OF MAKING SHORT PUTTS

Short putts are no different from tee shots or fairway bunker shots. They all count the same toward your score—and they are all more successfully executed the more confidence you have in doing them well. Confidence comes with an unconscious commitment to the process, along with repeated success. So practice short putts. See if you can make three in a row at three feet, four feet, five feet and six feet. If you miss, start all over. It gets you in the habit of feeling pressure and making a lot of putts. That's a good combination.

TIRED OF LIP-OUTS?
TRY SPLITTING THE TEES

Place two tees in the ground on either side of the hole. If you can get putts to fall without touching the tees, you've dialed in your aim with extra precision.

In 2002 at the Verizon Byron Nelson Classic,
Shigeki Maruyama won his second PGA Tour title
by holing a series of clutch putts in the final round.

Want to Make More Long Putts? Put a Good Roll on the Ball

PAY ATTENTION TO SHAFT ANGLE

You can make a perfect read and stroke a putt right on line, but if the ball takes a big hop off the putter at impact, as in the "No" photo at right, you lose speed and accuracy. That hop can happen if you hit your putts with the puttershaft angled backward at impact, which increases the loft. In this regard, a putt is really no different from any other shot you hit. The goal is to keep the hands moving ahead of the putterhead through impact, as in the "Yes" photo below right. The ball will hug the grass and roll more consistently and predictably.

FACTOR WIND SPEED INTO PUTTS

One of the hardest things to do on a windy day is putt. Believe it or not, even a 10 miles per hour wind is enough to influence a putt, especially when it's downhill. Be aware of the wind's direction before you putt and try to factor that into speed and line.

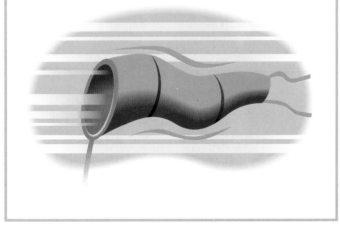

NO

YES

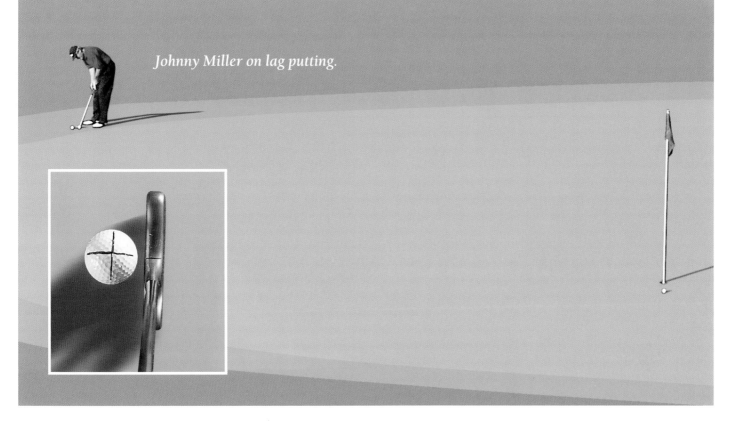

Johnny Miller on lag putting.

ON LONG PUTTS, SOLID CONTACT IS CRITICAL

On putts of 40 feet or more, you're forced to make an unusually long backswing. That makes it difficult to contact the ball solidly. Try this: Draw intersecting lines on your ball, and align them with the sweet spot of your putter. Keep your head still and focus intently on making precise contact. You'll cut your number of three-putts in half.

TRY THIS
ANTI-SKID DRILL

An effective way to keep putts from skidding is to stick a dowel rod into the ground so it's angled upward and toward the target, as shown here. Now place a ball under the rod at the halfway point and make a putting stroke that starts low and finishes high, tracing the angle of the dowel. The low-to-high stroke should get the ball rolling sooner—not skidding—to the cup.

Chuck Cook on "rolling your ball."

Put the Finishing Touches on Your Putting Game

SAVE STROKES BEFORE YOU START YOUR ROUND

Pre-round practice can be a key to breaking 80, and putting practice comes first. Practice your lag putting for at least 10 minutes. Your goal is to eliminate three-putts. You should consider three-putting as bad as a whiff. Almost inevitably on the first or second hole you're going to have a 40-foot putt, so be ready to two-putt early in the round from any distance. Phil Mickelson has a trick on long putts that you might try. He takes one practice stroke that he knows will be too short, then another that will be too long. Then he finds the middle ground for his actual stroke.

DO EVERY PUTTER A FAVOR: FIX YOUR PITCH MARKS

An 80s-shooter is a golfer who hits a lot of greens from far out—and who makes lots of pitch marks. It's the mark of a good golfer, so be proud of those craters. Just be sure to fix every ball mark you make on the green. Always carry a pronged divot tool in your pocket. Insert the prongs behind the pitch mark and push forward and up. Then tap the spot down with the sole of your putter. Use the tool as often as you can.

Jim McLean on warming up.

PRACTICE SHORT PUTTS BEFORE YOU PLAY

Don't overlook practicing three- and four-footers before a round. You'll face more of those under pressure situations than any other kind, and missing one feels like a missed chance.

STRUGGLING WITH THE FLATSTICK? RANDY SMITH SAYS 'MIX IT UP'

Until recently, I had pretty conventional opinions about putting. If a student was searching for a style, I'd teach a very standard setup. But after seeing the success one of my students had with cross-handed putting—when nothing else before had worked at all—I changed my mind.

Pick a style and type of putter you're comfortable with. That might mean going cross-handed or left-hand low, as in the photo on the left; going left-handed; or going with a long putter, or mid-length "belly" version. Whatever helps you make a consistent, repeating stroke will give you confidence— the key element in good putting. Putt with what makes you happy!

CROSS-HANDED

LEFT-HANDED

LONG PUTTER

Eliminate Those Final Wasted Strokes With a More Precise Stroke

PRACTICE PRECISION

Making good contact is just as important in putting as in full swings. A well-struck putt starts rolling quickly with minimal skid, and stays on track. Try the quarter drill to improve your putting: Stack two quarters behind the ball. As you stroke the putt, focus on hitting the equator of the ball, gliding over the quarters underneath. Do this from 5, 10 and 30 feet, and you'll roll the ball well.

PRACTICE WITH A GOAL OF EXTRA REFINEMENT

As an 80s shooter, your practice routine should be stringent. Be productive with your time. Have goals, such as making 25 three-foot putts in a row. You'll improve while learning to deal with pressure situations that will help in matches.

FIRST-AID FOR YOUR STROKE

To ensure that you're hitting your putts squarely, frame the sweet spot with rubber bands or bandages. That way only on-center hits will advance the ball on-line.

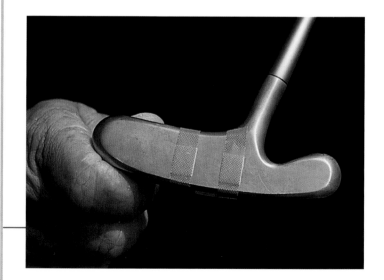

GET A LINE ON YOUR AIM

To break 80, you need to convert your good approach shots into par saves and birdies. From 10 feet and in, precision in direction is more important than precision in distance. Practice your directional control by using a string drill or chalk line. You can buy ready-made string putting training aids at most golf shops. You can buy a carpenter's chalk line at most hardware stores, for about $4. Find a flat area on the practice green and snap a 10-foot chalk line back from the cup. The putt can be slightly uphill or downhill, but should not have any sidehill break. You may need to snap the string several times to make a clear line. Then with a marker, draw a straight line on a ball.

Align the ball's mark along the chalk line. Then set your putterblade behind the ball so it is perpendicular

Hank Johnson on precision.

to the ball's mark. With a smooth, accelerating stroke, and your eyes directly over the chalk line, stroke the putt so the mark stays in line with the chalk line as the ball rolls into the hole. On the course, use the same line on your ball and imagine a chalk line in the direction you want the putt to start.

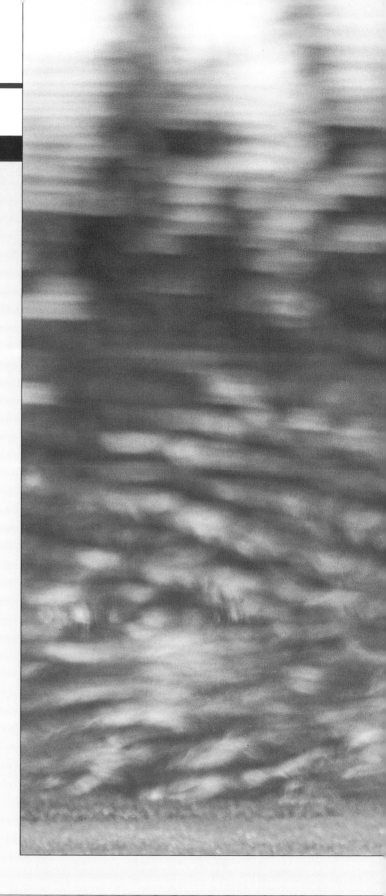

by Jill McGill, LPGA Tour

MY FIRST TIME

♦ ♦ ♦

I was on swim teams as a kid, so in the summer I would practice for two hours in the morning, then lounge around the pool the rest of the day. My mom gave me the choice of playing golf or going home and pulling weeds. It was a no-brainer.

To get me a little more excited about the game, my parents started giving me monetary incentives—a quarter for hitting a green or a dollar for making a par. The rewards got progressively bigger for bigger achievements—breaking 100 or breaking 90. (Wait, I won't get my '93 U.S. Amateur title taken away, will I?)

Anyway, I was 12 and playing at my parents' club, Cherry Hills in Denver, and I needed to make a par on the last hole to break 90 for the first time. We get to the green and there must have been 150 people right there, outside the clubhouse for a wedding reception. I've got a 30-foot, uphill, right-to-left breaker that I have to make to shoot 89. I roll it in, and all these people from the wedding party start cheering, and I'm jumping up and down. It was my first gallery. I went straight home to collect my prize.

After getting her start in golf at age 12, this Denver native won the 1994 U.S. Public Links Championship to go along with her '93 Women's Amateur title. A two-time All-American at the University of California, McGill has earned more than $1 million in prize money since joining the LPGA Tour in 1996.

Chapter 8

BUNKER SHOTS

Once you've mastered the technique of hitting it out of the sand, no bunker will seem a "hazard," just another shotmaking opportunity.

BUNKER SHOTS

Getting Out of the Sand

Many golfers, especially those new to the game, fear bunker shots more than any other shot in golf. The reason? Hitting the ball out of the sand requires a technique unlike any normal shot you make. It's the only shot in golf where you don't actually want to hit the ball. To get the ball out of the sand, you have to hit the sand first and allow the club to slide under the ball, propelling it out on a cushion of sand.

The key is to have no fear when you step into a bunker. You can't worry about leaving your next shot in the sand or hitting it over the green. You have to trust your club, your technique and yourself.

Once you master the basics of bunker play, you'll be able to fine-tune your technique to get the ball close to the hole. For better players, the ability to get up and down from a greenside bunker consistently is more than just a stroke-saving skill. It can give you the confidence you need to fire at the flag from long distance and take full advantage of the kinds of scoring opportunities that can lead to best-ever rounds.

Previous spread: David Duval blasts out of a sod-faced pot bunker on the Old Course.

Confidence is the key to getting the ball out of the sand. To improve, says top teacher Gale Peterson, learn to trust your club, your technique and yourself.

How to Get It Out of the Sand in One Shot

FOCUS ON THE SAND, NOT ON THE BALL

The beauty of bunker play is that you don't have to be as precise with your contact as you do when hitting from the fairway. In essence, it's a deliberate fat shot. Prove it to yourself by dropping four or five balls in the sand. Hit each one in quick succession, focusing on a spot a couple of inches behind each ball. That's where you want the club to enter the sand. Play the ball slightly forward in your stance so that the lowest point of your swing occurs slightly behind and under each ball. Now step back and examine the divot holes. You'll see they vary. Because of the margin for error the sand allows, so long as you accelerate the club through the sand you'll still get good results. Make impact closer to the ball, and it will travel farther in the air but have a lot of spin. Hit a little farther behind the ball, and it won't travel as far in the air but it will run more once it lands.

Ernie Els on the basic bunker shot.

WHAT'S THE RULE?

In a bunker, you cannot remove natural objects like pine cones, sticks or even dead snakes. They are considered "loose impediments" and are part of the hazard you have to play from. You can remove manmade objects, like paper cups or cigarette butts. You also cannot ground your club or take a practice swing and touch the sand—but you already knew that, didn't you?

THE BOUNCE FACTOR

The sand wedge is your best ally in the bunker. To know why, take a look at the bottom of the club. Notice the big bulge of metal just behind the leading edge? That is referred to as the "bounce," or the degree the sole angles away from the leading edge. Most sand wedges have 8 to 15 degrees of bounce, more than any other club in the bag. The bounce causes the club to skim through the sand just underneath the ball, rather than dig deep into the ground. It's a lot like a duck landing on a pond. The bird's webbed feet, angled upward, skim across the water. The feet never dip too far below the surface. That's exactly what you want the sole of your sand wedge to do as it enters the sand behind the ball.

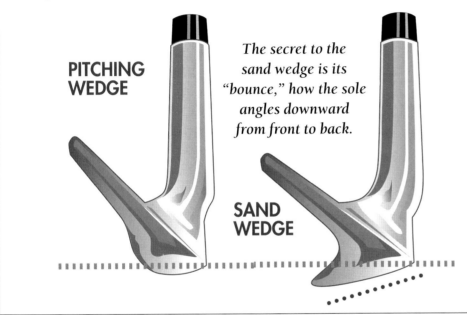

PITCHING WEDGE

The secret to the sand wedge is its "bounce," how the sole angles downward from front to back.

SAND WEDGE

GET SET CORRECTLY WITH THE SAND-BOX DRILL

The relationship between stance, swing path and clubface is very important in greenside bunker shots. Try this: Draw four numbers in the sand and divide them into quadrants as shown. (The horizontal line should be pointing at the target and parallel to your shoulders and feet.) Place a ball in the center and stand so your feet are in boxes 3 and 4 and the clubface is open, angled toward box 1. When you swing through, the club should travel from box 2 to box 3. This outside-to-in path, relative to the target line, is ideal.

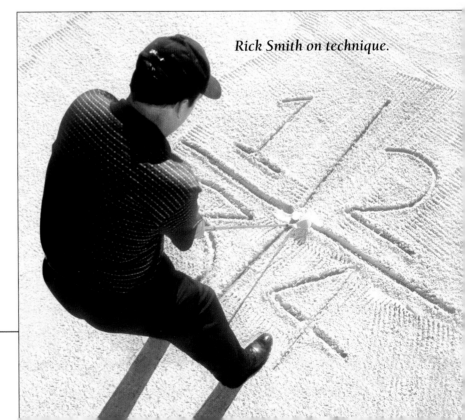

Rick Smith on technique.

Still Stuck in the Sand? Keep Your Technique as Simple as Possible

DRAW A LINE IN THE SAND

Most golfers are taught to play bunker shots by setting up to the ball with an open stance and an open club-face, then swinging along an out-to-in path. But that's not the only way to get safely out of the sand. Some golfers have more success when they use the same setup with their sand wedge as for a shot played from the grass. That is, their stance is parallel to the target line and the clubface is square, or perpendicular, to that line. The only difference is in ball position, which is more forward, in line with the left foot. This "normal" bunker swing is especially effective for golfers who use a specialty sand wedge featuring a wide flange and added bounce.

To see if this simplified sand shot for you, build a learning station in a practice bunker like the one shown here. Draw a line in the sand extending from an inch inside your left heel, then place the ball in a small circle just in front of that line. Square your stance and clubhead to your target. Your goal is to make a divot in front of the line, under your left shoulder. Focus not on the ball but on removing the sand from the circle. If the ball is anywhere inside that divot, the shot will turn out fine.

DON'T CHOKE DOWN

You might have heard that you should choke down on the club when you dig your feet into the sand. But think about it: You don't change where you grip it when the ball is on a tee, so why change it when you dig in? Take your normal grip on the club and simply focus on getting the club to enter the sand on the downswing, two or three inches behind the ball.

REMEMBER TO PRACTICE BUNKER SHOTS BEFORE YOU PLAY

Before a round, most players hit balls on the range and then stroke a few medium-length and short putts. That's not enough. Among other things, you should also hit some chips and definitely some bunker shots. Most players never practice sand shots, but you need to find out the texture of the sand on the course that day: Is it firm? Is it soft? Bunker practice will give you confidence when you get in that first bunker—which often happens on the first hole.

Butch Harmon on bunker practice.

Ernie Els Swing Sequence: The Basic Bunker Shot

FINE-TUNE YOUR TECHNIQUE AND LEARN FROM THE BEST

When I was a kid growing up in South Africa, I learned a lot by watching Gary Player (*below*) and David Frost. Gary's a great bunker player in all respects. Frosty is, too, and from him I saw how very still he is with his legs and how he uses only his upper body, especially his right arm. I still watch guys' technique on television, and continue to learn things even today. I guess it's my turn now to serve as a role model, so take a close look at the sequence photos here. You may not need to get up and down from a greenside bunker to win a major—as I did at the 2002 British Open—but a well-played bunker shot may be the only thing between you and your best round ever.

Gary Player was Ernie Els' role model for bunker basics.

Getting the Ball Out of the Sand and on the Green Every Time

SPLASH SAND ONTO THE GREEN

Know that hitting through sand requires three times as much swing as a shot of the same distance played from outside the bunker. So don't be afraid to make an aggressive swing. Play the ball opposite your front heel, and don't allow the clubface to rotate closed through impact. Practice splashing a thin, footprint-size divot of sand (and the ball) toward the target. The acceleration should be so smooth it's almost unnoticed. The last thing you want to do is jab at the ball.

Jim McLean on acceleration.

DON'T BE A MACHO MAN

The object of golf is to get the ball in the hole. Putting out of a bunker may not be considered macho or stylish, but it's effective if there is no high lip to clear. Unlike a regular putt, lean the shaft slightly forward and don't ground the putter.

Rick Smith on following through.

VARY YOUR FINISH TO IMPROVE ACCURACY

The length of the backswing in a bunker shot isn't nearly as important as the follow-through. Simply put, the longer the shot, the more complete the follow-through needs to be. Here's a good guide: For short shots, the club should get to about knee high. For medium-length shots, the club should finish chest high. And for your longest bunker shots, a complete follow-through may be necessary.

THE MENTAL SIDE

DR. BOB SAYS PLAY AS IF YOU CARE—JUST NOT ABOUT SCORE

Maybe we'd all play better if we got our scorecards at the end of our rounds instead of the beginning. Thinking about your score rarely helps you execute shots. Instead, you have to learn to play as if you don't care about your score. That's different from playing as if you don't care. Get excited and focused—that's fun. But focus on preparing to make a solid swing, not on how it affects your score. Leave the card in the locker room. Focus properly and you'll have no trouble remembering every shot after the round, because there will be fewer of them.

A Fairway Bunker Doesn't Have to Mean a Dropped Shot to Par

Hank Haney on fairway bunkers.

HIT IT THIN OFF SAND

From a fairway bunker, play the ball a bit farther back in your stance than normal and try to hit at the equator to pick it off the sand. Thin is better than fat.

CHOOSE YOUR WEAPON CAREFULLY IN FAIRWAY BUNKERS

Being able to visualize ball flight is crucial when deciding what club to use from a fairway bunker that has a lip between you and your target. Your No. 1 priority is clearing the lip. Resist the urge to cut it close with a longer iron to move the ball farther down the fairway. Pick the club that gets you out of the bunker with a healthy margin for error. It's likely to be a five-iron or above.

HOW DAVID LEADBETTER CHARTS YOUR POTENTIAL

Look at your "potential" score rather than the actual score you happened to make that day. This breeds confidence, and it shows you what you're capable of doing. You also need to be objective when looking at your weaknesses. Analyzing your worst-hole scores gives you an idea of where to make improvements. In the example below, Bill shot 104. To calculate his potential, add his best scores on nine holes (five par 4s, two par 5s and two par 3s). Now multiply that number (44) by two (88), adding 10 percent (9) for the "rub of the green." Bill's potential? He could easily shoot a 97.

Hole	1	2	3	4	5	6	7	8	9	Out		10	11	12	13	14	15	16	17	18	In	Tot	HCP	Net
Par	4	3	5	4	5	3	4	4	4	36		4	4	5	4	3	4	3	4	5	36	72		
Handicap	16	10	8	2	6	18	12	4	14			11	15	1	5	17	7	13	9	3				
Bill	5	4	7	5	6	4	8	7	5	51		5	4	8	6	6	7	5	6	6	53	104		

WHEN TO TAKE YOUR MEDICINE

To break 90, avoid big scores. A good rule: never attempt a heroic shot after a bad shot. If you're in deep trouble, just take your medicine and play the simplest shot to safety.

Getting It Pro-Style Close—From Any Distance and Any Kind of Lie

MASTER THE DOWNHILL BUNKER SHOT

Even good players are intimidated by a bunker shot from a downhill lie. Before visions of balls zooming over the green start dancing in your head, relax. If you can keep your shoulders on the same angle as the slope of the hill, you can play this like any other bunker shot, with the ball forward in your stance. Point your left toe out, toward the target, and kick your right knee in toward the ball. Swing along the slope, and follow-through. The ball will have a lower trajectory, but it will get out of the bunker.

Dean Reinmuth on tricky lies.

RAKE LIKE A PRO

A well-executed shot isn't the end of your business in the bunker. For pro-style raking, use this technique: Skim across the sand with the teeth of the rake as usual, and then use the other side of the rake to smooth the area flat. No golfer likes to hit out of a footprint or the deep furrows created by a rushed rake job.

HOW TO HANDLE AWKWARD LIES

How the ball is sitting in the sand will affect how you play the shot. To play from hardpan (the ball sitting on top of firm sand), you don't want to expose too much of the sand wedge's flange. If you do, the club will bounce off the firm surface and you'll skull the ball over the green. Keep the clubface square, as you would for a normal shot off grass, and hit from a slightly open stance. From a "fried egg" lie (the ball half-buried in its own crater), you need more digging, so close the clubface. Put more weight onto your left foot and attack the ball from a steep angle.

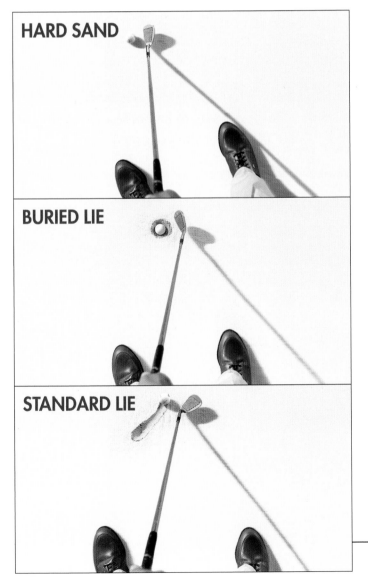

HARD SAND

BURIED LIE

STANDARD LIE

'SLAP' THE SAND WITH YOUR RIGHT HAND

The swing on the greenside bunker shot is dominated by the right hand. First weaken your left-hand grip, so that the back of the left hand faces the target. This helps keep the left hand from taking over and closing the clubface through impact. (Always remember to open the clubface before you take your grip.) Keep your weight left, but quickly bring the right hand up, then "slap" the sand with your right hand and follow through. To ingrain the feeling of the right hand in control, practice bunker shots holding the club with the right hand only. You'll be surprised at the results.

Butch Harmon on the role of the right hand.

Some Bunker Shots Really Are Difficult. Here's How to Hit Them

TAKE THE BITE OUT OF LONG GREENSIDE BUNKER SHOTS

When you hit the sand two to three inches behind the ball, you get about one-third the distance you'd get from hitting the same shot from grass. If you hit your sand wedge 90 yards, you can hit a standard sand shot about 30 yards. But a longer bunker shot? You have two options to get it close, says Tom Ness: You can either hit closer to the ball and take less sand, or you can switch clubs. To hit closer to the ball, adjust your ball position an inch or so back toward the center of your stance. Just be careful. Cut it too close and you'll hit the ball first, sending it over the green. Clubs with less loft will allow you to take a full swing from sand and carry the ball farther. Make sure you have enough loft to clear the lip. And know that clubs with less loft have less bounce and can dig into the sand. Play the ball slightly forward of center and swing to a full finish.

MAKING THE MOST OF A BURIED LIE

This shot is one of the few that require wholesale changes in your setup. First, keep in mind that no matter how you hit this shot, it will come out low and run when it hits the green. Set up with your weight on your left leg and the ball in the middle of your stance. That way, the club will be tilted so the leading edge will dig. Hit a couple inches behind the ball. Let the club bury in the sand, splashing the ball out.

USING A FAIRWAY WOOD FROM LONG RANGE

When you're in sand or a waste area far from the green—and you don't have much lip to deal with—it's often a better option to hit a fairway wood instead of a long iron. Just open the face of the wood slightly, as shown here, and aim more left. Opening the face lowers the back edge of the club, which will slide atop the sand. If you do hit behind the ball, the club won't dig, it will skip into the back of the ball, and you'll still get the ball out of the bunker and down the fairway.

by Paul Azinger, PGA Tour

MY FIRST TIME

✦ ✦ ✦

Unlike a lot of guys on the PGA Tour, I wasn't a natural-born golfer. When I arrived at Brevard Community College in Cocoa Beach, Fla., in the fall of 1978, I had a hard time breaking 80 on consecutive days, which is why I spent my freshman year as the No. 3 player on Brevard's "B" team. My first college coach, Jim Suttie, is the one who introduced me to teacher John Redman. Those two are largely responsible for my growth and success as a player.

I'll never forget the first time I broke 70. I needed a par on the 18th hole, a short par 5. After reaching the green in two shots, I stood over a 50-footer for eagle knowing I could three-putt and still shoot 69.

I got down in two for a 68. When I excitedly told Redman what I'd shot, he didn't seem at all surprised. Maybe he didn't have any idea how far I'd come in such a short period of time, or maybe he did know but didn't want me to think I'd peaked as a player. Either way, it was a sign of great things to come.

A lot of what I've been able to accomplish goes back to that round in 1980. More than 20 years later, the memory remains a fond one, not so much because I shot 68, but because I was up to the task, providing me with the confidence I needed to take my game to the next level.

For Paul Azinger, breaking 70 for the first time was a sign of great things to come. Azinger became a PGA Tour star and a Ryder Cup hero, holing this dramatic bunker shot on the 18th hole in the 2002 competition.

Chapter 9

TROUBLE SHOTS

*Knowing how to recover
from difficult lies and get the
ball safely back in play can
save you strokes in every round.
The secret is sound thinking
and proper execution.*

TROUBLE SHOTS

Getting the Ball Safely Back in Play

Between the teeing ground and the putting green you will encounter a variety of obstacles, hazards and other impediments to getting your ball in the hole in the fewest strokes possible. It's what makes the game so difficult to master and so endlessly challenging.

For players at any level, getting out of trouble with the smallest number of wasted shots is the best way to shave extra strokes off your score. The key is learning how to make the correct decision based on your ability and the difficulty of the shot you face. First, examine your lie. How is the ball sitting? Will your swing be obstructed by a low-hanging branch or exposed tree root? Next, consider where you want your next shot to take place. What club and swing will best allow you to get from a tough spot back to safety? Learn how to hit higher-percentage recovery shots and you'll meet your scoring goals quickly, without a major swing overhaul. While you're at it, keep in mind that golf is just a game. Remember to have fun, and be creative when facing trouble.

Previous spread: After an errant drive, Sergio Garcia muscles one out of "the hay."

*Even the best players,
like Phil Mickelson,
can find themselves
in recovery mode.*

Making the Right Decisions to Get Out of the Wrong Places

GET BACK TO THE SAFE GROUND—NOW!

When you're trying to break 100 for the first time, a bogey is a great score, and it should be your goal. If you hit a shot behind a tree or a tall bush, think hard before you try going over it. If you have any doubt about clearing the obstacle, don't compound your mistakes—and bury your ball in the brambles. Pitch out to the safety of the fairway. You can still make bogey.

Dean Reinmuth on playing safe.

CHART YOUR COURSE

Reading a course guide is just like plotting a driving route on a map. Find the most direct—but smoothest—way to get to the green. Know where the trouble is so you can plan ahead to avoid it.

MINIMIZE YOUR MISTAKES BY SELECTING THE RIGHT CLUB

We've all been there—racked up a triple bogey. After we do it, we could kick ourselves for not playing the hole differently. So let's eliminate those bad decisions.

When you find your ball nestled in the rough, don't automatically grab a fairway wood. Judge your lie. If you see blades of grass between the clubface and the ball and the rough is four inches deep, you won't be able to maintain much clubhead speed through impact. You're better off taking a club that's got more loft. Do what you must to get back in the fairway.

Wendy Ward on club selection.

KNOW THE RULES

WHEN TO SAY WHEN: DECLARING YOUR BALL UNPLAYBLE

Declaring a ball unplayable is sometimes your best option. If you don't think you can chop out to safety, take the drop and cut your losses. The Rules of Golf allow a player to declare his ball unplayable at any place on the course except when the ball is in a water hazard. If the player deems his ball to be unplayable, he shall, under penalty of one stroke:

• A: Play a ball as nearly as possible at the spot from which the original ball was last played; or

• B: Drop a ball within two club-lengths of the spot where the ball lay, but not nearer the hole; or

• C: Drop a ball behind the point where the ball lay, keeping that point directly between the hole and the spot on which the ball is dropped, with no limit to how far behind that point the ball may be dropped.

If the unplayable ball is in a bunker, the player may proceed under Clause A, B or C. If he elects to proceed under Clause B or C, a ball must be dropped in the bunker.

Here's the good news: The ball may be cleaned when lifted under this Rule.

Getting Your Ball Out of the Thick Grass Far From the Green

HOW TO HIT A FAIRWAY WOOD FROM THE ROUGH

Rather than trying a 3- or 4-iron, use one of the lofted metal fairway woods or hybrid woods to get out of rough. The shape of the head, the loft of the club and the low center of gravity elevate the ball more easily and increase your margin for error.

Every lie that gives you distress immediately signals that you should move the ball back a little in your stance. Although it's still slightly forward of center, play the ball so your hands fall naturally ahead of it at address. This encourages a steeper backswing, which in turn promotes more of a descending blow at impact, as with a middle-iron. The result is that you will hit more ball and less grass, with the loft of the club helping get it airborne.

KNOW YOUR EQUIPMENT

WOODS FOR TALL ROUGH

Lofted fairway woods, especially the 5-, 7- and 9-woods, are easier to hit than long irons, because the clubfaces are bigger and the ground cushions the sole to soften those slightly fat hits. The clubhead on a long iron will get eaten up by the rough, but the bigger, wider head and lower center of gravity of a higher-lofted fairway wood can cut through some higher grass.

Rails on the sole help the club slide through grass.

DON'T TRY TO BE A SEVE

Play out of mistakes wisely. Instead of attempting a Seve Ballesteros shot that requires untold hours of practice to pull off successfully, just get in the fairway. The smartest shot is the one you can make with the lowest margin for error. If two wedges will get you home, don't try the high-risk 3-wood from the rough. Never attempt a shot during a round that you haven't practiced first on the range. Practice hitting shots from thick rough, not just from perfect lies off artificial turf or on a tee.

FIRM UP YOUR GRIP FROM THE THICK STUFF

Sometimes the smartest play from deep rough is a pitch shot back to the short grass. Select a high-lofted iron, firm up your grip and deliver a downward blow. Remember to accelerate the club through impact.

Do a 'Rough' Analysis to Hit Your Irons From Bad Lies

SWING STEEPER IN THE DEEP GRASS

The first thing to remember about playing from the rough is to minimize the time the clubhead drags through the grass before it gets to the ball. That means swinging on an upright rather than a sweeping path. From a decent lie in the rough, play the ball slightly back in your stance (*below*), and open the clubface a little bit at address to offset any chance of the grass grabbing the hosel and turning the clubface closed.

CLEAR THE VIEW—CAREFULLY

When in trouble, check your lie and make it look better—e.g., carefully remove twigs from around the ball. The more ball you see, the better.

READ THE LIE TO DETERMINE YOUR SHOT

The severity of your lie in the rough will tell you how to proceed. From a good lie (*above left*), use your normal setup and keep the clubface square. Since some grass will get between the face and the ball at impact, the ball will come out with less spin and probably fly longer than normal. A shot from a mediocre lie (*middle*) is the most common, and should be played with the ball slightly back in the stance and the face slightly open. For really bad lies, (*right*), where most of the ball is nestled down in the grass, open the clubface dramatically and make a steep swing, bringing the club down almost on top of the ball to gouge it out.

THE MENTAL SIDE

DON'T MOURN THE SHOT THAT GOT AWAY

You should not feel happy about making bad shots, but use your "bad-shot quota" as comfort. If you're an 18-handicapper and make a bad shot, you can figure it's just one of 18 bad shots you can expect to make over the course of an 18-hole round. Remember what Bob Rotella always says: Golf is not a game of perfect.

How to Factor Wind Into Your Shotmaking Equation

HOW TO BEAT THE BREEZE ON THE GREENS

If your pant legs are flapping, then the wind is affecting your putts—especially on fast greens. To steady your stroke, stand a little wider at address. Also, don't ground your putter, because the wind can come over the top of the clubhead and create a vacuum that sucks the ball back onto the clubface—a one-stroke penalty. Suspend the clubhead just off the ground about three-quarters of an inch away from the ball.

Nick Price on putting in the wind.

Butch Harmon on playing in the wind.

HOW A CROSSWIND CHANGES YOUR PLANS

With shots into the green, turn the ball into the wind so it holds its line and lands softer. Off the tee, don't fight it; let the ball ride the wind. Never aim where a straight shot will get you into trouble, though.

CHILLY DAY? USE A VEST

Most golfers striving to break 90 already have restricted swings. A coat or sweat-shirt on a cold, windy day doesn't help. To dress warmly, wear a long-sleeve shirt under a sleeveless vest, for freer arms.

AN EASY WAY TO JUDGE WIND SPEED

At 10 miles per hour, the treetops move consistently; at 20 mph, your shirtsleeves or pant legs move, and at 30 mph, you can't keep your hat on. If the wind exceeds 30 mph, it's a different game. Just keep the ball in play, even if it means hit-ting a sort of bunt with a long iron rather than your typical high, pretty golf shot.

IS THIS A 2-CLUB WIND?

The simplest way to factor wind into your full shots is to use this formula: For every 10 mph into the wind, take one more club than usual. For downwind shots, take half a club less than usual. Keep your strategy conservative, but swing assertively.

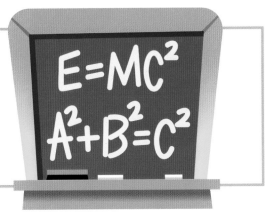

Avoiding Big Numbers by Avoiding Trouble in the First Place

MARKERS CAN MISLEAD

When setting up on the tee, make sure you square yourself to the target and not the tee markers. Markers may be placed to direct you to the right or left of your intended target. It's helpful to stand back from the ball and survey the terrain before you put your peg in the ground.

KNOW YOUR LIMITATIONS...

If you want to break 90, it is imperative that you put the ball in play off the tee. Hitting it O.B., in a hazard or in deep rough can cost you more strokes than even a very good short game can recover. On long par 4s and par 5s, maybe you'd be better off hitting something in the fairway and playing form there, rather than hoping to hit a career tee shot with your driver. Know your limitations. You can own those longer holes by taking advantage of your handicap. Learn to net-par those longer stroke holes, and your scores and your handicap will go down.

...AND SCORE WITH THE GAME YOU HAVE

The quality of your bad shots is at least as important as the quality of your good shots. If you're trying to break 90, you're an 18-handicapper or higher. Use

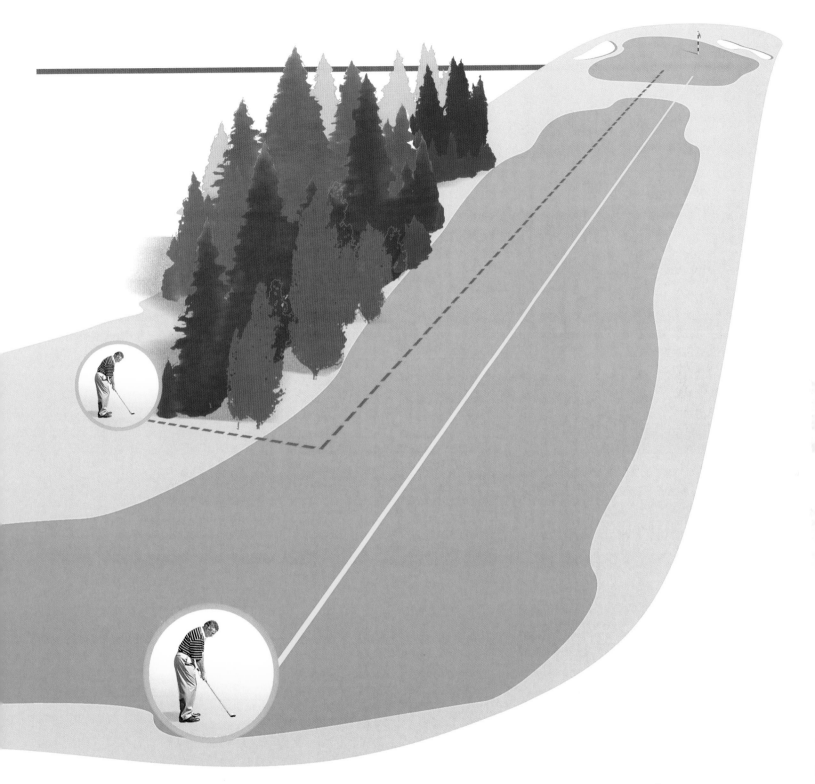

those strokes to set strategy. On a 400-yard par 4 like this one, remember that you're lying minus-1 on the tee. Decided how to use that free swing. You can swing for the fences with your driver, and hit it wildly, leaving yourself a 250-yard dogleg par 4 from behind the pine trees. Or you can take out the 3-wood and slap it down the fairway, leaving you a 200-yard par 4 from the middle of the fairway. It's pretty easy to see which strategy is going to yield a lower score.

*Tiger Woods pitches out of snarly iceplant—
a troublesome hazard found throughout
Pebble Beach Golf Links and other courses
along the Monterey Peninsula.*

Learn When to Go for the Flag and When to Play Safe

AIM TO TAKE THE BIG NUMBER OUT OF PLAY

On par-3 holes shorter than 185 yards, your natural impulse is often to aim right at the flag and fire. On a hole like the one here, you should be taking the trouble out of play. If you aim at the flag and pull it or leave it short, you're all wet—and staring at a double bogey. A better play is to aim at the right edge of the green. A straight-shot is on the green, and a pull will end up in the middle of the green. If you do bail out right and short, you'll have an easy chip.

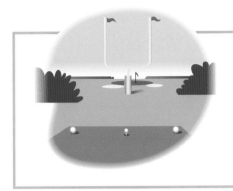

THREAD IT THROUGH THE UPRIGHTS

Don't focus on what you're trying to avoid—in this case, thick bushes left and right of your target line. Instead, pick an object—a leaf, clump of dirt or whatever—two feet in front of the ball on a safe line and use it as your intermediate target. Commit and hit it over that spot.

REDUCE RISK AS MUCH AS YOU CAN

In the situation I'm facing here, not many good things can happen. If I try to hit my pitch shot right of the flag, I'll have to deal with that big hump in front if I want to run the ball up. If I want to carry the ball all the way to the hole, I'll have to make sure to get over the back side of that mound, or else it'll kick off the back of the hill and I'll be chipping from behind the green. The best play is to go over the trees and shoot for the exposed, safe left side of the green and take my chances with the putter. I can take all of the problems out of play.

Hank Haney on risk.

KNOW HOW TO GO HIGH OR LOW

Controlling the fight and height of your shots is a crucial part of becoming a good player. If trees are too close, as in this photo, a punch shot is a good call. Move the ball just right of center in your stance and hit what amounts to a hard chip shot. Keep your wrists firm through impact and finish low. If you've got enough room to go over, open the clubface slightly and play the ball forward in your stance. Swing a little harder—otherwise you'll lose distance because of the open face and extra height.

To Become a 'Player,' Learn How to Hit Good Shots From Oddball Lies

*Dean Reinmuth
on stability.*

WHEN THE BALL IS ABOVE YOUR FEET

Depending on the severity of the slope, you must make incremental changes in your swing. Stand slightly farther from the ball than you would for a level lie (*ball at left, below*). Grip down on the club to adapt to the hill and reduce the chance of hitting it fat. Take a practice swing to see where the club meets the ground. Maintain your posture through the swing. This stance encourages a hook, so aim to the right.

Judy Rankin on hanging lies.

BALANCE IS THE KEY TO UNEVEN STANCES

The driving range and the tee box are the only places where you'll never have to hit a ball that's sitting above or below your feet. On the course, you've got to make adjustments. To hit a ball from an awkward position—the ball significantly below your feet, for instance—you have to keep your balance throughout the shot. Any instability during the swing will cause you to straighten up before impact—you body's reflexive action to keep from falling over. And on this kind of shot, if you lose your spine angle, you'll hit a weak dribbler to the right. Hold your weight against the slope by flexing both knees a little more than normal. Before you hit the real shot, take a few practice swings to feel where the club should brush the ground.

Johnny Miller on downhill lies.

DOWNHILL: TRY TO HIT THE BALL LOW

Instinctively you may try to help the ball into the air by swinging up on it. That's the kiss of death, because you'll hit the ball fat or thin almost every time. Instead, play the ball back in your stance, swing parallel with the slope, and let the shot come out low. Some people will advise you to take one more club when hitting off a downslope, but stick with the club you'd normally hit. You won't carry the ball as far as you would if you were hitting off a level lie, but the net distance will be the same.

EARN RESPECT WITH YOUR SHORT GAME

Who doesn't envy a good chipper from awkward lies? Play the ball *way* back in your stance. For poor lies, play it off the shoelaces of your back foot. It will ensure a crisp, downward hit on the ball every time.

Look at Obstacles as a Chance to Get Creative—and Have Some Fun

BE A KID AGAIN

The time she's spent with junior golfers has led Janet Coles to believe there's a lot to learn from a child's approach to the game. For instance, when Ariana Patterson (*below*) sees something such as a water hazard, she doesn't worry about hitting into it. Instead, she looks at the hazard as a "fun" obstacle to overcome. Kids swing without fear because they haven't yet learned what fear is on a golf course. If only we could all think this way. Overcome your fears; be a kid again.

CONSIDER ALL YOUR EXIT STRATEGIES AND CLUB OPTIONS

When you're in trouble, you've always got four directions to hit the ball: forward, kind of forward, sideways and backward. You've also got three different trajectories you can choose from: high, low or in between. That gives you a total of 12 different possibilities for getting out of trouble.

After you've quickly analyzed all 12 of your exit options, it's time to pick a club. Remember, you've got 14 clubs in your bag, and you can use any one of them whenever you want. Use your imagination. Here, for example, I've decided that my best choice is to putt the ball down the cartpath. Why not? In this case, the ball ended up right next to the green!

John Elliott Jr. on using
your imagination.

The Go-for-Broke Option: How to Save Par From the Clutches of Disaster

GOT NO STANCE?
HIT THE BACKWARD RECOVERY

You hear a lot of talk about playing conservatively, opting for the sure bogey to avoid the big number. That's fine, but this dull strategy also limits your chances to make par or birdie. Especially in match play, where the most you'll lose is a hole, there's no harm in trying the hero shot.

For example, when your ball is resting against a tree or rock, the smart play can be to take an unplayable lie, a one-shot penalty. Here's a go-for-broke option: Using a 9-iron, turn over the club but keep your regular grip, hitting the ball cross-handed. Take a narrow stance and keep a still body, focusing your eyes on the back of the ball. Swing mainly with your arms, straight back and through. Your goal is to put the ball on the green or back in the fairway, but your priority is simply to get out of trouble.

Hank Haney on the hero shot.

DON'T BE AFRAID TO HAVE FUN

No matter how poorly you play, remember that golf is a game, and you are doing this for fun. Remember, this isn't your living—laugh at your bad shots.

SPLASHING THE BALL OUT OF WATER

A miraculous save from what seems to be an impossible spot is one of the most exciting shots in golf, not to mention one of the most memorable.

For example, when your ball's on the edge of a water hazard, you can play it so long as the top portion is above water. Use a sand wedge and hit behind the ball, literally splash the ball out of the water, just as you would an explosion shot from a greenside bunker. Don't quit on the shot. Remember, as in a bunker you can't ground the club at address.

by Nick Price, PGA Tour

MY FIRST TIME

◆ ◆ ◆

In July 1974, when I was 17, I traveled outside Africa for the first time. My destination was the South Course at Torrey Pines in San Diego, where I had been invited to participate in the Junior World Championship. I had little idea of what to expect.

At the Junior World, I competed against 256 golfers from 28 countries in the 15- to 17-age group. I wasn't thinking about winning, just putting up a good show. The best anybody from Rhodesia had done was to finish in the top 25. I was hoping to finish in the top 10.

An opening round of 69 tied me for the lead, and I followed that with two 72s to take a three-shot lead into the final round. In the end I won by four shots after a final-round 74, but not before I had some problems. On the 17th hole, I drove into a bunker and hit my second up into a tree, where the ball stayed. I went on to make a triple-bogey 7.

The win was a big deal at home. I had won against some top young players such as Gary Hallberg, John Cook and Hal Sutton. When I got home, people made such a big thing of it that I was actually embarrassed.

In San Diego, I had managed to get the ball into the hole by accepting the ups and downs. In my second-round 72, I made five bogeys, three birdies and an eagle, clear evidence that just about anything could happen when I was on a course. I struck to a game plan. I knew that it was important to accept any bad patches; who knew what might happen on the next hole?

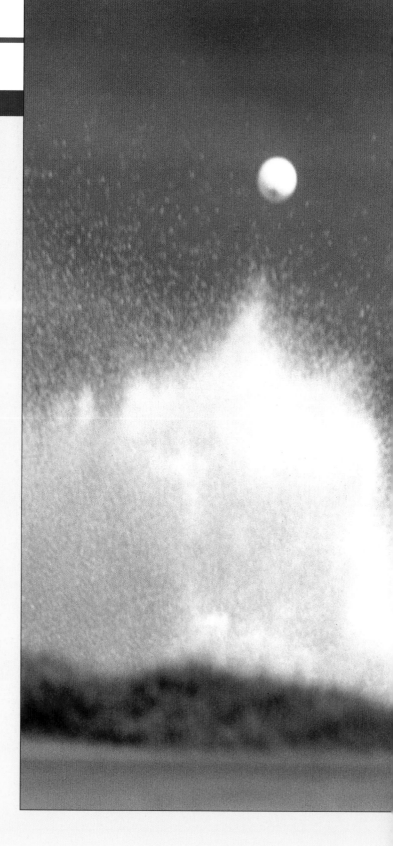

GETTING THE BALL SAFELY BACK IN PLAY

Chapter 10

FITNESS

*As the top pros are proving,
athleticism in golf is an asset.
The proper physical conditioning
will help you break through
your scoring barriers.*

FITNESS

Boosting Your Strength and Flexibility

Generations of players were told that golf and exercise didn't mix. Conventional wisdom held that any attempt to increase your fitness would lead to a decrease in feel. Golf, the experts maintained, was not an athletic sport, it was a game of skill, of touch.

The first big-name golfer to challenge this myth was Gary Player, whose commitment to strength training, increased flexibility and proper nutrition was long ridiculed as eccentric, even crackpot behavior. But as athletes began using advanced training techniques to achieve performance breakthroughs in other sports, it was inevitable that the benefits of proper physical conditioning would be applied to golf.

Today the specially equipped fitness vans that accompany the major professional tours are crowded all week long. Virtually every top tour pro now follows a fitness regimen designed with his or her physical needs and goals in mind. The good news for the average amateur is that you don't need a fitness van or personal trainer to get in better shape—all that's required is a commitment to embark on a fitness program tailored to your specific needs, and the discipline to keep at it. If scoring your best is your goal, then getting more fit for golf is a necessary step.

Previous spread: Justin Leonard hits the beach to keep his golf game in top shape.

To take their games to the next level, tour players like David Duval now utilize a wide variety of training regimens, including yoga.

Make Better Swings by Stretching Your Golf Muscles

FOR BETTER GOLF FITNESS, START AT THE BACK

Let's be honest. If you can't perform the most basic of back stretches, you cannot make a proper golf swing. Try this one: Lie on your back with your legs extended. Raise your knees toward your chest, holding your kneecaps or shins and keeping your knees as close together as you can. If you can raise your knees to your chest and hold that position for the length of one long breath, you are more flexible than 90 percent of the golfers who visit my fitness center for the first time.

Randy Myers on stretching your back.

YES

NO

A GREAT GOLF STRETCH—
IF YOU DO IT RIGHT

Most trainers cringe when they see golfers put a club behind the shoulder blades and start twisting back and forth. No fitness expert has ever proved how this helps your back. Instead, stand in your normal address position, grab each end of a golf club and extend it horizontally in front of you. Turn back and through as if you were making a golf swing—feel the stretch in your spine and shoulders. Hold the back-swing and finish positions for a few seconds.

TIME TO GET ATHLETIC

If you've hit a tennis ball, baseball or hockey puck, you know the importance of balance and posture. When you swing a golf club, be an athlete.

How to Put a Cart to Good Use—and Why You're Better off Walking

LOOSEN UP YOUR SHOULDERS

There's not much of a health benefit to be gained from riding in a golf cart, but before your round starts, you can use a cart for an important stretch. Stand next to the canopy post, your feet shoulder-width apart. Grab the post with both hands, keeping your arms fully extended. Pull away from the post and hold the position for the length of one long breath, then repeat facing the opposite direction. This will stretch your shoulders and back and get you ready for the first tee.

John Elliott Jr. on walking.

DRINK UP, BUT WISELY

Nothing is better than water to quench your thirst. Drink it before, during and after a round. You don't need to overdo it, but the more you perspire the more you need to drink. (And don't be fooled by dry, desert-like heat that doesn't leave you dripping.) Staying hydrated helps you keep your focus and finish strong.

A word of caution: Ice-cold water on a hot day sounds good, but it shocks the system and slows the digestive process. Drink at least four or five cups of water when you play, but make sure it's closer to room temperature than the freezing point.

WALK FOR POWER

Playing golf requires you to have a certain level of athleticism. You can't make a strong, athletic move through the ball if you aren't in shape. One of the best ways to strengthen your body—especially your lower body, the base of your swing—is to walk while you play golf. For even stronger legs, carry your bag. It will help your game in the long run. Besides, sitting in a golf cart can does more harm than good to your back.

Becoming Physically Fit Pays Dividends Both On and Off the Course

GET FIT TO FINISH STRONG

Physical fitness should become a priority when you reach your 40s. The more physically fit you are, the stronger you'll be mentally, especially late in the round. Elite golfers work out two to five times a week, focusing on cardiovascular exercises, like riding a stationary bike. Most also do some strength training, along with regular stretching. You're not out to build muscle with a fitness regimen; you want to maintain your strength level, flexibility and muscle tone in an effort to prevent injury. Prevention is always better than the cure. To that end, get regular checkups from a physical therapist, and see a dermatologist every few months to make sure you're not developing skin cancer, a real concern for golfers who spend a lot of time out on the course.

BETTER, BIT BY BIT

Just as increasing your strength and flexibility is a long-term process, rarely will a player make a quick leap from a 120-shooter to the 90s. Instead, strive to knock at least a stroke off your score each round.

*Nick Price
on staying fit.*

KEEP YOUR MIND IN THE HERE AND NOW

You're at the level where every little factor can save a shot. That includes staying focused on the business at hand. Don't let a wandering mind keep you from executing the best you can. Learn to pace yourself, not only physically but mentally. In a typical round, you spend only 16 1/2 minutes actually preparing to hit and hitting the ball. Like Fred Couples (*below*), learn to use your down time to relax, enjoy the scenery or rehearse a simple swing key.

How to Stay a 'Flat-belly' and Score Your Best Into Your Senior Years

CRUNCH YOUR WAY TO STRONGER ABS

Gary Player gets a kick out of seeing fellow tour players who used to ridicule him for exercising now doing it themselves. Better late than never. Even if you start at age 50 or 60, you can strengthen your body. One of the most effective exercises is the stomach crunch, which strengthens and tones the abdominal muscles. He does as many as 1,000 crunches a day, some when he gets up in the morning, some after his round, more before he goes to bed. Gary does them three ways: legs wide and stretched along the ground; knees up, with feet on the floor; and a more strenuous variations in which the legs are together and raised off the ground. Keep your hands behind your head, and don't raise your lower back fully off the ground.

WATCH WHAT YOU EAT

Avoid big, hefty meals before you play, and watch your caffeine intake. The guy who orders two hamburgers, french fries and a beer at the turn has got no chance to score his best.

DO THE SKIER'S SQUAT
FOR BETTER POSTURE

When a boxer's skills start to deteriorate, they say the legs go first. The same thing can happen with golfers. If your legs weaken, you lose the support you need, and you develop posture problems at address. To keep your legs and lower back strong, do the skier's squat on a regular basis. Lower into a sitting position, your heels flat and your thighs parallel to the ground. Hold your arms in front of you and keep a slight arch in your back (*inset photo, above*)— don't hunch over. Try to hold this position for 30 seconds or more. Now feel some tension in those same muscles when you set up to the ball.

Don't Have Time to Stretch Before Your Round? Make Time

IN A RUSH? TRY THE 'PARKING-LOT' STRETCH

Try to get to the course a little early before you play and spend 10 minutes stretching your muscles. You'll feel less tension on the first tee—and you'll be less stiff the next day. Really in a rush? Try this stretch: When you pop the trunk to get your clubs, put a foot up on the bumper to stretch your groin. Repeat with the other leg.

Randy Myers on pre-round stretching.

MAKE FULL USE OF THE LOCKER ROOM

Opportunities to stretch can be found at almost every turn. Before your round take a few minutes to stretch your hamstrings (*above left*) and your lower back (*above right*). Leg strength and flexibility is often ignored by golfers, but getting those hamstrings worked out is a must, especially for golfers who walk. Extend each leg on the bench, and don't rock as you lean forward to grab your toes. If you can't reach your toes, try for an ankle. For your back, the best thing to do is lean forward and give your thighs a hug. This stretches the back and elongates the spine.

ONE FOR THE ROAD

You can do this back stretch before a round if you're short on time. But it's especially useful after you play or practice. Rest your hands on top of the cart to support your weight while bending over.

'Stay on the Ball' With Workouts Designed Especially for Golfers

TO GET MORE FLEXIBLE, HAVE A BALL

First things first: Buy an inflatable stretch ball. Available at most sporting-goods stores, this low-tech piece of equipment gives you the added benefit of having to maintain your balance while performing a number of different exercises. Here, Randy Myers is doing a great catchall exercise that improves the strength and flexibility of the abdomen, shoulders and arms. It even helps the lower back. Grab a light weight, a gallon water jug or whatever is handy, and try to do a motion similar to a sit-up while keeping your arms extended. You'll really feel this in your abs.

CLUBS MUST FIT YOUR PHYSIQUE

Clubfitting is important to the better player. If you're built like Joe Pesci and use clubs designed for Clint Eastwood, you'll never improve.

SHRUG OFF TENSION

Tension is the root of many swing problems. Be sure to avoid shrugging your shoulders. Before you swing, consciously unshrug your shoulders and you'll make smoother, more rhythmical and more consistent swings.

MASTER THE ULTIMATE GOLF EXERCISE

This exercise is typical of what we ask an elite golfer to do. Holding two dumbbells, kneel on top of a stretch ball, trying to maintain your balance. Once you can stay on the ball, let your arms hang by your sides and then try raising your arms to shoulder height. Repeat the motion. You stay on the ball by using a number of golf muscles; your arms get a workout from the weights. Do this on a cushioned surface, and always consult a physician before embarking on any fitness program.

Take Your Game to the Next Level With a Pro-Style Training Regimen

COMPOUND YOUR STRETCHES

Exercises that allow you to work two or more parts of the body at the same time are doubly effective. With this stretch, you can work the hips, back and shoulders. Here's how: Lie flat on the floor and grab one arm and pull it across your body. Now rotate your hips so your belly button is pointing in the opposite direction of the extended arm. Bend your legs so both knees are touching the ground; try to hold this position without lifting your shoulders. Some elite golfers start their day with this exercise. You can even do it in bed. How convenient is that?

STRENGTHEN YOUR CORE

Studies have shown that swinging a driver creates the same amount of muscle force a weightlifter generates in lifting 90 percent of his maximum weight. One of David Duval's main objectives is to strengthen the core of his body from the ground up and the inside out. To that end, he uses the Pilates Hundreds exercise to develop the stability he needs to generate more speed and power with less effort.

Here's how to do it: Lying on your back, raise your legs as you curl your head and shoulders off the floor, focusing your eyes on your navel. Do 5 reps of five inhales and 5 exhales—hence the name, Hundreds.

YOU CAN LEARN A LOT FROM PILATES

Pilates was developed during World War I to help rehabilitate injured soldiers. Today, it's a fitness methodology that improves balance, strength and flexibility—and it's really good for golfers. The exercise at left is Pilates 101. The objective is to move your spine into the same angle as when you address a golf ball. From a sitting position, extend your arms forward and spread your legs wide, your toes pointing up. Now simply lean forward and hold the position for a deep breath.

DON'T BOUNCE

It used to be that fitness instructors taught bouncing, ballistic movements in stretching. Today, we are teaching slower, consistent movement with an emphasis on being in the correct posture. So if you want to stretch your back, don't bounce. Gradually stretch until your reach your limit.

After a Solid Foundation of Strength, Add Speed-of-Movement Training

HOW PLYOMETRICS CAN HELP FINE-TUNE YOUR BODY...

Popularized by East German athletes in the 1970s, plyometrics has been a standard part of Olympic training regimens for decades and has also been adopted in recent years by athletes in other sports that require fast, explosive movement, like golf. The goal is to develop controlled power through a sequential firing of the muscles.

For speed-of-movement training to be effective, you first have to develop adequate muscle control, range of motion and strength. That's a key point: Forcing out-of-shape muscles to respond to the kinds of quick, powerful contractions required by plyometrics is just asking for injury.

One basic plyometric exercise for golfers is the lunge drill. As Justin Leonard demonstrates, leap sideways form left foot to right foot and back for 30 seconds. "Sit" into your buttocks, keeping your knees flexed and your weight between the balls and heels of your feet.

...AND HOW WORKING OUT CAN HELP YOUR SWING

In the lunge drill shown below, Justin is building up his thighs and his butt muscles. That's where your quick body turn comes from, as well as your clubhead speed. In the golf swing, as the upper body turns through, it's got to be braced by a stable yet powerful lower body; the right side of the rear end has to really turn back into the ball. The stronger those big muscles are, the better they can fire on command.

You can't rotate your upper body with the greatest speed possible unless you've developed sufficient flexibility and rapid-fire strength in the torso and legs. The more flexible and strong those muscles become, the more you've got a coil effect, as opposed to just twisting your hips without storing power in the right side in the backswing. Working out on a regular basis with plyometrics and other speed-of-movement exercises not only can pay off with more distance, achieving this level of fitness can also boost your stamina level, allowing you to go deeper into the round, remaining fresh to the end.

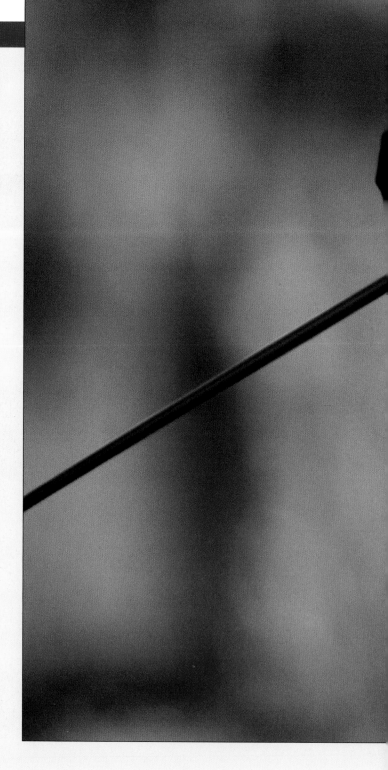

By Al Geiberger, Champions Tour

MY FIRST TIME

✦ ✦ ✦

It was Friday, June 10, 1977, and it was hot. The Danny Thomas Memphis Classic was being played at Colonial Country Club, one of the toughest we played on the PGA Tour. It also was not in very good shape, the Bermuda greens stubbly and the fairways thinned out so badly that we were playing preferred lies. So I really didn't wake up thinking I was going to be the first PGA Tour player to shoot 59.

Starting on the back nine, I was only two under through my first five holes when the peanut-butter crackers arrive. My friend Bob Schreiber brought them; I used to—and still do—eat peanut-butter sandwiches during the round for quick energy. I ate four or five crackers on the spot, and I'm sure Bob thinks he's responsible for the 59, because I played the next seven holes in eight under par.

I really tried for the PGA Tour record of eight consecutive holes under par, but I parred the fourth hole. Still, trying to break the record took my mind off my eventual score and got me past the choking point.

My birdie putt on the last hole was one that I knew where I wanted to play it the instant I looked at it. I hit the putt and it just dove right in the center of the cup, and all hell broke loose.

Al Geiberger captured 11 PGA Tour titles over 25 years, including the 1966 PGA Championship and his record-breaking performance at the 1977 Danny Thomas Memphis Classic. Since joining the Champions Tour in 1987, "Mr. 59" has won 10 times. He still carries a peanut-butter sandwich in his bag.

THE EDITORS

Golf Digest's Playing Editors and Teaching Professionals work closely with staff editors to create instruction articles that are clear, concise and applicable to golfers of all abilities. Here are the editors who co-authored the original "Breaking 100, 90, 80" articles.

SCOTT SMITH
Director of Instruction Scott Smith joined *Golf Digest* in 1996. The chief editor of this book, Smith has written articles with Jim McLean, David Leadbetter, Ernie Els and other *Golf Digest* Playing Editors and Teaching Professionals.

MATTHEW RUDY
Instruction Editor Matthew Rudy has been an editor at *Golf Digest* since 1999. He is the author of *Golf Digest's The Swing: Secrets of the Game's Greatest Players*, *Breaking 90 with Johnny Miller* and *The Complete Idiot's Guide to Golf*.

Editor Scott Smith gets a tip from David Leadbetter. Right: Rich Beem celebrates winning his first major.

ROGER SCHIFFMAN
Roger Schiffman is Vice President/Managing Editor of *Golf Digest*. Since 1979, he has written articles with many pros and teachers. He is co-author of *The 3 Games of Golf* with Hank Johnson, and *Perfectly Balanced Golf* with Chuck Cook.

RON KASPRISKE
Associate Editor Ron Kaspriske has been with *Golf Digest* since 2000. He has worked with many of the game's top instructors and tour professionals, including David Toms, Phil Mickelson and Hank Kuehne.

MIKE STACHURA
Mike Stachura has been an editor at *Golf Digest* since 1992. He has co-written articles with Nick Price, Mark O'Meara and Dr. Bob Rotella, among many others. He currently serves as Equipment Editor and is the author of two golf books.

TOPSY SIDEROWF
Associate Editor Topsy Siderowf has been with *Golf Digest* since 1982. She has done instruction stories with Judy Rankin and other LPGA players, in addition to directing the *Golf Digest* course survey projects and junior rankings/awards.

GUY YOCOM
Senior Writer Guy Yocom has produced many instruction articles since joining *Golf Digest* in 1984. He has collaborated on books with four U.S. Open champions: Tiger Woods, Johnny Miller, Corey Pavin and David Graham.

CLIFF SCHROCK
Cliff Schrock began with *Golf Digest* in 1984 and has written numerous instruction and historical articles. Now Editor of the *Golf Digest* Resource Center, overseeing the magazine's archives, Schrock has written four books on golf.